THE 123 APPROACH TO FITNESS

THE 123 APPROACH TO FITNESS

BY ARRAN KNIGHT
+ DAVID MICHEL

Arran Knight Pilates
St Patricks Studios
Dundee Street
Wapping E1W 2PH

This edition 2023
1
First published in Great Britain by Night Owl London 2023

ISBN 978-1-3999-4155-6

Printed and bound in Latvia

All reasonable care has been taken in the preparation of this book, but the information it contains is not meant to take the place of medical care under the direct supervision of a doctor. Before making any changes in your health regime, always consult a doctor. While all the practices detailed in this book are completely safe if done correctly, you must seek professional advice if you are in any doubt about any medical condition. Any applications of the ideas and information contained in this book is at the reader's sole discretion and risk.

Editor: Kay Halsey
Photographer: Drew Paul
Designer: Emily Voller Design
Illustrator: Hannah Fleetwood

Foreword

In my capacity as Head of Medical services at a Premier League football club in England and having worked in the elite sports environment in both the UK and North America, I have witnessed the importance of engaging athletes with appropriate injury prevention and progressive rehabilitation regimens. My experiences working in the NHS and the private healthcare domain, in addition to my own personal sporting experiences, have also taught me that the same principles of education and engagement are essential tools when working with recreational athletes and indeed any patient suffering with musculoskeletal pain and associated dysfunction.

I have been fortunate enough to work alongside likeminded, holistic practitioners in Arran and David during my work with elite athletes in professional sport. Their input has been invaluable in helping with problem solving complex rehabilitation cases and also in designing injury prevention programmes for elite athletes. The rapport that was developed from such interactions helped facilitate compliance from athletes and created positive behavioural change in both the short and longer terms.

I am a big believer in the interplay between the mind and body when it comes to sporting and exercise participation across diverse groups of people. To neglect one aspect in my role as a Chartered Physiotherapist will be to the detriment of a successful outcome in terms of patient quality of life and health promotion. Arran and Dave are both keen proponents of the same philosophy and by investing time and energy in looking after the mind and body, you will undoubtedly become a more resilient and confident human being.

The 123 Approach to Fitness book is an excellent adjunct to set you on your way towards optimal health and fitness. No matter your age or physical condition, the ethos of the book is to facilitate your skill acquisition in terms of how to prepare, perform and recover from a structured series of exercises that will help increase your physical activity level and promote cardiovascular health in alignment with UK Government and NHS physical activity guidelines. The user-friendly, hybrid philosophy articulated by Arran and Dave stems from their respective Pilates and Yoga philosophies, with the format of the book creating an autonomous approach towards strength, stretch and soft tissue release techniques that will serve to optimise your fitness.

With a clear and simple layout, pictorial guides, space for your own note keeping and reflection within each chapter to guide you along the way, this book will be the perfect companion to help you achieve your desired fitness goals.

At this point, I would like to refer to a phrase that adorned the London Marathon finishers medal that I completed, which has stuck with me on both a personal and professional level. It read 'Success in life is a journey, not a destination.' I have no doubt that by reading this book you will be embarking upon the first stage of the journey towards creating a more resilient physical and mental outlook for the future.

Good luck on the journey!

Richard Collinge
MBA MSC MCSP SRP

Success in life is a journey, not a destination.

Contents

▲ Section 7

FURTHER THOUGHTS

Introduction

In this book, we want to offer you a new perspective on how to approach exercise. We want to show you that you don't have to follow the current exercise trends. That you can transcend those trends and, in doing so, you will feel more comfortable, confident and relaxed in your body when moving.

We have spent the last decade shaping world-class dancers and being part of elite Premiership footballers' return from injury to full-match fitness. In doing so, we have refined our movement strategies and approach to body conditioning to help them harness and manage tension in their bodies, and be in the best physical condition they can be in. We have taken the best of Pilates and Yoga and combined them with release work to develop a cutting-edge approach to our bodies when approaching specific movement forms. We would like to offer you the tools to become your own personal trainer, stretch specialist and massage therapist all rolled into one.

When exercising, body conditioning programmes, like we offer here, are often missed out. For example, many people decide to begin running one day with no knowledge of, or thought for, how they might prepare their bodies. As a result, they injure themselves and all that good intention goes to waste. On the flip side of that, there are your typical Yoga and Pilates advocates who are diligent with their bodies, but that is all they do because it feels safe to them. Pilates and Yoga are exercise forms where you have a lower likelihood of injuring yourself, but they avoid cardiovascular exercise to the detriment of your overall health. Scientific evidence is clear and explicit that we need to have an element of cardiovascular exercise to keep our organs, and therefore bodies, healthy. We know from our work with elite sports people and dancers that conditioning programmes help them to get the most out of their bodies' cardiovascular system in a consistent manner. Our 123 method aims to promote both types of exercise by laying out how best to use specifically chosen body conditioning strategies to support your chosen cardiovascular activities.

We aim to combine a safe and supportive approach to exercise that you can adapt with an activity-specific focus. We want to give you the tools to manage your own body. The tools that elite athletes and dancers find so essential with theirs. We'd also like you to understand the value of combining strengthening exercises, stretching and release work – as we and many elite athletes do. We offer an integrative self-help guide, which gives you a memorable and easy-to-use method when approaching exercise. We call this our 123 Approach.

This simple and practical model will act as a guide for you when exercising. It will teach you how to:

- Harness and manage tension in your body.
- Feel more comfortable, confident, in touch and relaxed when moving.
- Become more energetic through learning how your body functions.
- Apply these principles to some of your everyday movements.
- Apply these principles to running, cycling and swimming.
- Apply warm-up and recovery strategies to your chosen activity.

You can be any age, and in any condition, to apply these principles. We want you to understand how to become pain and tension-free in how you move. We will teach you strengthening exercises, stretching techniques and release methods that will leave you feeling like an expert at how to maintain your body.

With the current pressures to look a particular way or obtain a specific level of fitness, you can often be left feeling uncomfortable in, and feeling out of touch with, your own body. We believe that by managing the tension in your body we can help you get into the most functional condition you have ever been in. In turn, you will look your best and feel the most energetic and pain-free you have felt in your life!

'Working with this approach has made my body feel better than it has done in years!'

Graham Norton

'The model makes sense on a number of levels of body movement. This approach has been of real value to some of our Senior and Academy players at West Ham United FC.'

Richard Collinge – West Ham United Head of Medical Services

'This is an excellent and simple approach to enhancing everyday movement patterns and allowing users to maximise their physical potential. Arran and Dave bring a huge wealth of experience, which is encapsulated and accessible to all, within this book, and enables anyone to learn and apply the core principles we use developing our dancers. Their approach focuses on strength, control and tissue mobility as key to all fundamental movement patterns in which to springboard pain-free functional movement or for excelling in sport.'

Karen Sheriff – Royal Ballet School Healthcare Manager

About us

Arran and David became friends after training together at **Northern School of Contemporary Dance** in Leeds. Having gotten a taste of the professional dance world from a national tour with Ballet Lorent, Arran left NSCD to study postgraduate Musical Theatre at the Royal Academy of Music. He performed with the Howard Goodall original cast of *A Winter's Tale*. He was also part of the cast of *Wicked*, the biggest-grossing West End Musical for 2010. After an injury, Arran discovered Pilates with Alan Herdman. He has worked as a Pilates instructor for the **Royal Ballet School for the past 11 years**. He has also spent the last two seasons as a Pilates consultant for the **Premiership team West Ham United**. He runs his own business – Arran Knight Pilates – in Wapping, London.

Dave completed the training, including the acclaimed postgrad company Verve, and went on to dance with **Retina Dance company**. After becoming more and more interested in Yoga, Dave retired from professional dance to train as a Yoga instructor. He now runs his business – David Michel Yoga – from Ramsgate, Kent.

The 123 Approach basic model

The 123 Approach is a simple concept. We believe that for bodies to function well and remain pain-free, we need to learn how to manage the tension in our muscles. You can do this using a combination of:

- strength building exercise (tension on)
- muscle stretches (slackening off)
- release work (resetting muscles to a pliable state) for when trigger points develop (Trigger points are a tender area in a muscle that causes musculoskeletal pain when external pressure is applied to it.)

We like a Triangle, as you will see when reading on. Here's the first we'll use to describe our idea of the 123 Approach:

Two of these areas are common:

- 1 Strength
- 2 Stretch

One of them is often left to people who work in the professional realms with their bodies. As such, it's often neglected:

- 3 Release

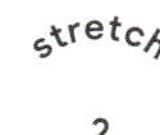

What is release work?

Simply put, release work is self-massage using small props like balls and rollers. In this book we will show you varying techniques for releasing various areas of the body.

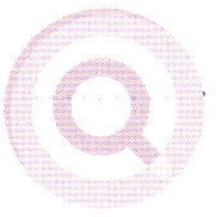

Spotlight: What happens in the muscle when you release it?

When you release a muscle, you increase the blood flow to the area you are working on. This scenario speeds up the delivery of nutrients to the muscles and disposes of metabolic waste, which can slow down muscle recovery and cause pain. When we use muscles repetitively, the muscle fibres can become stuck together, which reduces a muscle's ability to strengthen and stretch, and can lead to injury.

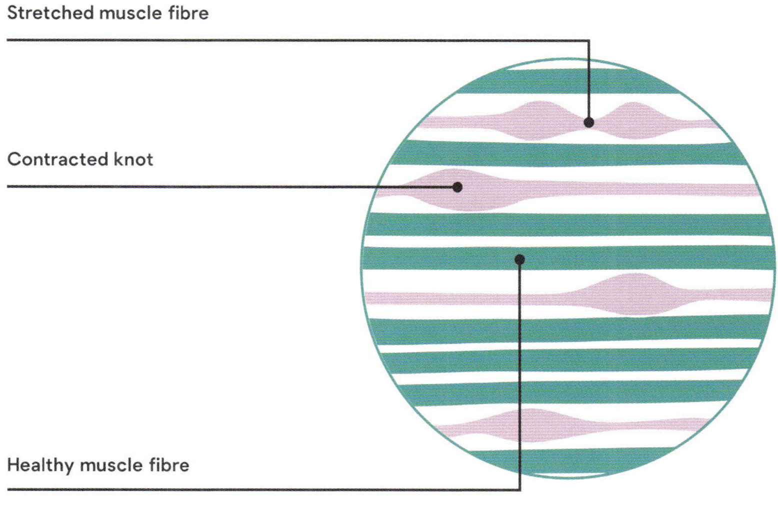

WHAT ARE THE BENEFITS OF RELEASING A MUSCLE?

- muscles and tendons relax
- potential to reduce nerve compression
- heart and breathing rate slow down
- decreased blood pressure
- can help improve digestive process (research inconclusive but positive)

Back to the Triangle model . . .

These three areas – 1 strength, 2 stretch, 3 release – are the cornerstone points of conditioning programmes for athletes the world over.

Now, the Andy Murrays of this world have the best massage therapists on hand post-match, or training session, to soften their muscles back to a state of relaxed tension. They have the best personal trainers helping them look at increasing speed, power and explosive effort. They often have someone to hold their leg up to stretch the hamstring. In short, elite athletes have a multi-disciplinary team of professionals to keep them doing what they do!

In working with the Royal Ballet School and helping to prepare dancers for the demanding world of elite ballet, these are common concepts. These strength, stretch and release strategies are also applied in elite Premiership football, and we have used them to positive effect at West Ham United. We are aiming to provide you with the same kind of approach that elite sports people and dancers use to maintain and get the most out of their bodies.

Our book aims to teach the average person these concepts to help them manage their own bodies themselves. With a little understanding of the principles in this book, we believe you can be your own Personal Trainer, Massage Therapist and Stretch Specialist. You can become your own multi-disciplinary support team! We will give you the information to support you to make informed choices about what warm-up strategies, cool-down programmes and body-conditioning exercises to use for whatever activity you decide to enjoy. We'll have you on the path of the 123 Approach to Fitness in no time!

Some useful information before we start

How to use this book

We recommend that you begin by really getting to know the basics. Try the strength, stretch and release work with your main muscle groups, building up a rhythm of exercise times throughout the week. Then watch and feel for the benefits.

Understanding the main muscle groups

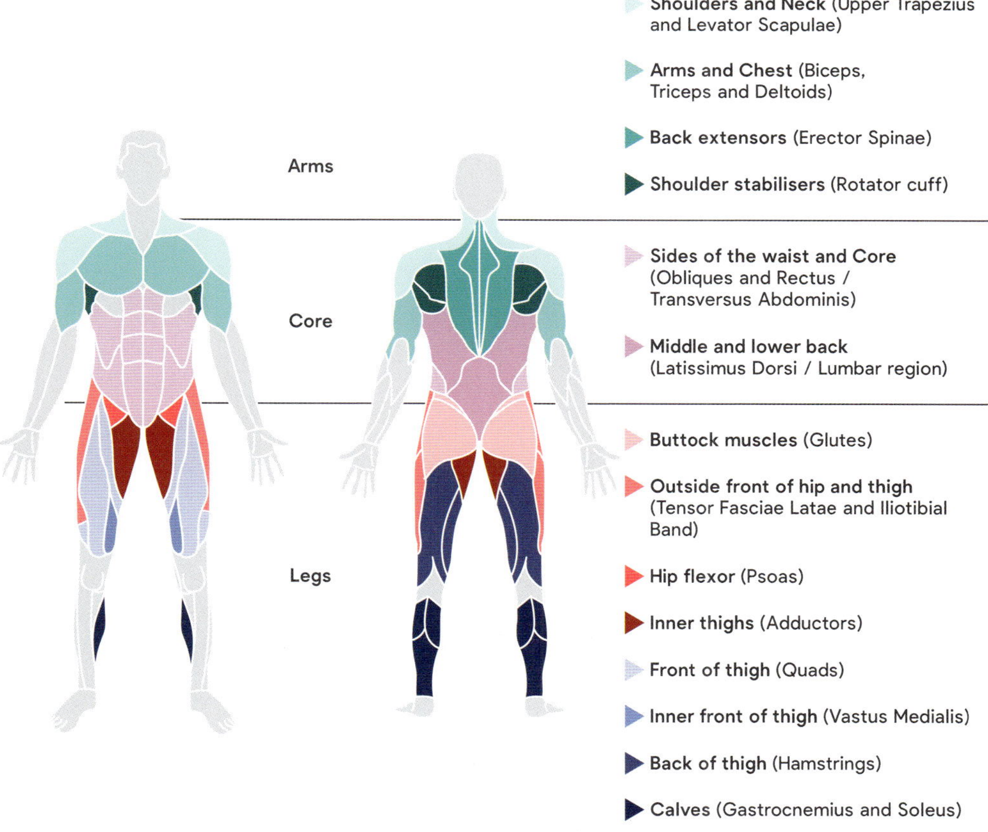

Ways to get started

Next, you could do one of three things:

- We have taken three forms of everyday movement: sit to stand, walking and reaching and rotating. One option is to rotate these three exercise programmes, and perform them on three separate days throughout the week. This will cover most of the movements that you perform in a day and, therefore, keep your body in good functioning condition.
- Alternatively, if there is one of those movements that you struggle with, you could go straight to that section and experiment with the exercises there to try to improve that movement.
- Lastly, if one type of the three cardio options that we offer a perspective on is your thing, then you could go straight to that section in the book. Once you get to know the exercises we suggest, you can then experiment with them and note the benefits when you next go for a run, cycle or swim!

The movements that we offer – sit to stand, walking and reaching and rotating – relate directly to the cardiovascular activities we have offered. So, sit to stand relates to cycling; walking relates directly to running; and reaching and rotating relates directly to swimming. The exercises from the respective movements progress onto the exercises for the cardiovascular activity. This allows you to develop your programme in an appropriate and coherent way.

Whichever way you choose to work with our models, we hope our message in this book comes across clearly – that our bodies like variety of movement. We would encourage you to get to know these exercises in whatever way you decide to enjoy and incorporate them into your daily routines. It might be that you then play around and experiment with other options offered here or put together your own programme for your chosen activity, based on your newly acquired knowledge.

Timings and equipment

In each section where we offer a group of exercises for a particular movement, such as running, we state how long the exercises will take when performed together, demonstrated by a clock with the number of minutes next to it. We also suggest what equipment you will need for each section (see pages 14–15 for a list of our recommended equipment).

Note: The timings of a collection of exercises work based on having your equipment ready.

5-minute programme

10-minute programme

Number of reps and time spent in positions

With reference to timings and the repetitions of exercises, we suggest the following:

- Each stretch should be held for 30–60 seconds (or 10–15 deep breaths). Some stretches go through repetitions if it is a movement-based stretch rather than a static hold. We will indicate this separately on each individual exercise.
- Perform 10 repetitions of every strength exercise, with the option of increasing this to 3 x 10 repetitions as the exercise gets more familiar.
- Release a muscle for as long as is needed for the discomfort level to drop from an initial pain threshold of 8 out of 10 until it reaches 3 out of 10.

Also, please note that we describe some exercises on one side, leg or arm only. Make sure you repeat it on the other side as well. We would not want to leave you off balance!

Spotlight

We will use this magnifying glass symbol to hone in on any bits of information that we think need more detail throughout the book.

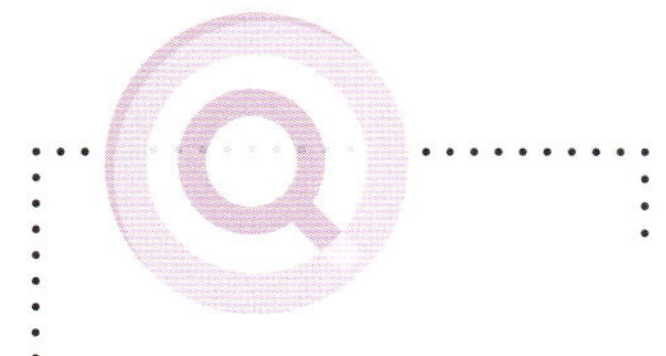

Summary

We will use this summarising symbol at the end of each chapter to encapsulate what we have covered.

Building up release work

When you first decide to release a muscle, it will be painful if you haven't done it before. We like to think of it as a pleasure-pain sensation, but it will certainly be uncomfortable. Our experience of release work is that the longer you leave a muscle without attending to it with release work, the more painful it will be. If you have an area that is chronically tight and you haven't released it before, it will take a few sessions to ease it off. We would suggest persisting with this, as you will notice the difference within a few release sessions. One suggestion is to use softer balls at first and build towards more solid balls. If you do begin with softer balls though, we would suggest not avoiding a progression onto more solid balls as the muscles will ease more quickly and thoroughly with the uncompromising integrity of a harder ball. A word of warning is to only go as hard as a lacrosse ball. Something with a little give in it is recommended. No cricket balls, please!

The four Ps

Having a thought process when exercising is important. We came up with the catchy four Ps to help. Purpose helps you understand what area you are targeting and why. Prepare helps you to consider your starting position. Perform ensures that you know how to execute the movement. And Prudence helps you consider body safety by looking out for what might be bad technique. We suggest you go through this checklist each time you execute an exercise. Before long you will do this automatically. At this stage links between exercises and body parts will begin forming in your chosen programmes. This will make you versatile and prepared to take on whatever you desire.

The convenience of home workouts

One of the things that we realised very quickly when embarking on careers as a Pilates instructor and a Yoga instructor was that exercise needs to be convenient. We know that from our own workouts. Having a space that is comfortable and pleasant to be in seems to us to be one less barrier to deciding to work out. We make sure the flooring is not too hard, so that when you're doing something like stretching glutes in a seated position, it doesn't press into the ankles. We recommend a thick carpet, so you don't have the hassle of putting out a Yoga mat. One of us even works on our hamstrings while at the bathroom sink brushing our teeth!

How often should you perform these exercises?

Whether you are the type of person who creates a lot of space in their life for exercise or you struggle to find time for looking after yourself, there is enough information here to keep you going.

You could, on the one hand, perform these exercises daily, or a collection of them that suit you. On the other hand, you might only do a set of exercises here that you like once a week. Our main thoughts are that it's important to get a balance of strengthening, stretch and release work, and to do some level of cardiovascular exercise to keep yourself functioning well and remaining healthy.

Either way, we suggest you start with whatever is manageable. If you need to start slow and build up that is fine. If you find yourself overexercising and injuring yourself a lot, get something that is at a level you enjoy and work out what is sustainable. If it's not working, strip things back a bit. It's important to see how your body responds to a new exercise programme. Let your body and the information in this book lead you.

Useful small equipment

We recommend the following equipment as essential, practical and comprehensive for all the exercises we suggest in this book. We have kept this list as minimal as possible to ensure it is storable and travelable. You will find fixing points for the TheraBand exercises in any household in the form of door handles, heavy table legs and radiator pipes. Failing that, you could always ask a friend to allow you to wrap it around their legs and return the favour!

THERABAND

A rubber band that stretches to provide resistance. This can be purchased with a variety of resistance levels that are colour-coded. We would recommend a blue colour as a good all-round resistance level.

STRETCH STRAP

This is a taut strap, much like a belt or dressing-gown cord, that can be used to assist in stretching.

ROLLER

This is a cylindrical piece of foam, which can be used for release work and strengthening work. They come in a larger form if you want something you can keep at home. We also recommend a smaller, more portable option to take with you wherever you go.

RELEASE BALLS

These are tennis ball-sized balls with a much harder texture, which do not lose shape over time. They can be purchased in a range of solidity, from soft to hard. We recommend beginning softer and working your way up to something firmer as you get used to them.

INFLATABLE BALL

This is what it says on the tin. The ball can be useful as a weight-bearing support or to provide resistance in certain positions.

BLOCK(S)

This is a small foam block that can be used to support body parts in particular positions.

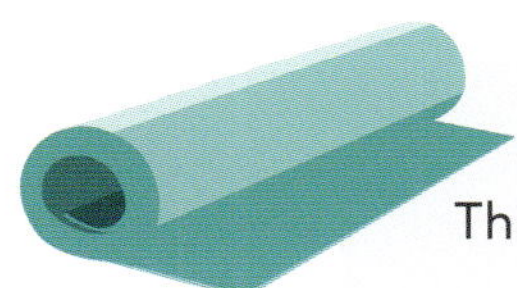

EXERCISE MAT

This is a mat that can provide comfort to lay on, and extra grip.

CUSHION

This can be a purpose brought pillow, or one from your bed or sofa.

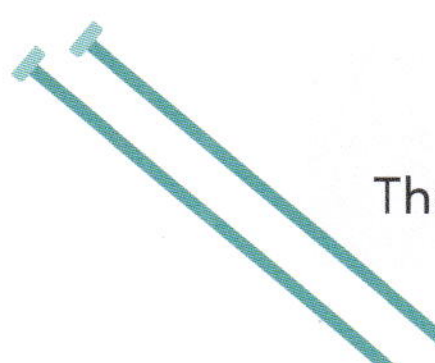

STICKS

These are wooden sticks that can be used to hold onto for balance.

We also recommend the following, non-portable two bits of kit for home use.

STOOL

This is used for some of the strengthening and stretching exercises and something can easily be acquired wherever you are. However, having a stool at home that is designated specifically for your exercises will make life easier when used on a regular basis.

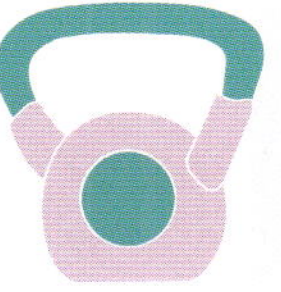

KETTLE BELL

This is an iron weight shaped like a kettle. It is common in most gyms and is useful for release work on the inner thighs from time to time.

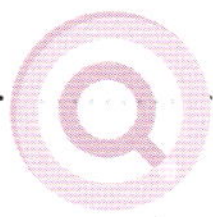

Spotlight: What is a neutral spine?

A simple description of a neutral spine is allowing the vertebrae of the spine to rest in their natural structural position, without any manipulation from muscles or body positional changes. So how can we demonstrate this practically?

Lie on your back with your knees bent. If you try to slide your hands under your lower back you should be able to get your fingers under there but not the whole hand, although this may vary depending on body type. If you try to tuck your pelvis, or curl the tailbone, off the floor, you should feel your lower back press into your hands. Now you could go in the opposite direction and increase the arch in your back, pulling it away from the floor. Both these movements take the spine out of a neutral position. The neutral spine lies somewhere in between.

Incidentally, another way to change your neutral spine would be to shorten one side of the waist, as if you were trying to bring one of your hips to the same shoulder. In either direction you would be taking your spine out of its neutral position laterally, although this direction is a less common issue.

Spotlight: What is a constructive rest position?

The constructive rest position is simply lying on your back with your knees bent and your feet flat on the floor, as described above. This helps to lengthen the spine and provide a place to start from in a lot of Pilates exercises.

Self-acceptance and your body

Now we have introduced our basic concept and laid out some useful information upfront, let's get started with developing these ideas! Before we do, we recommend you take a moment to check your mindset.

If we were to briefly imagine here a world where we just focused on our bodies functioning well, rather than their aesthetic form, what would it look like? Well, we would all feel a hell of a lot better about ourselves, we're sure.

We would accept the body shape that we have been given and not try to become something we are not. This would lead to wonderful benefits, such as developing real relationships with our bodies.

Our bodies talk to us through sensation. They give us such a lot of information through pain, fatigue, muscle growth, muscle wastage, our sense of energy and the list could go on.

It's important to begin to listen and to strive to maintain that conversation throughout our lives.

We do, after all, only get one body!

So, we invite you to go on a journey with your body. The first step is an internal one.

Here is a model to help with your thinking:

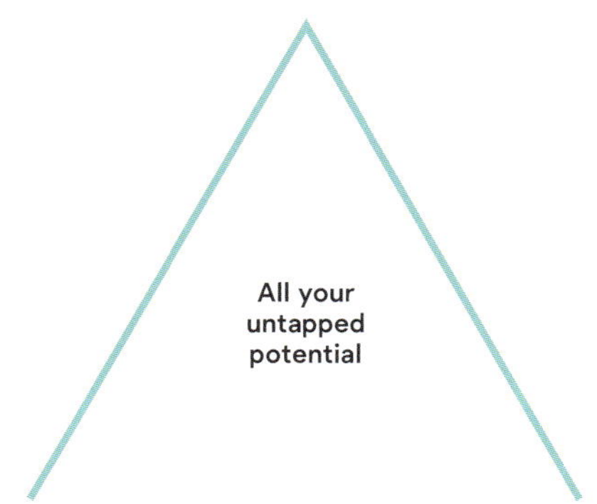

Your relationship with your body

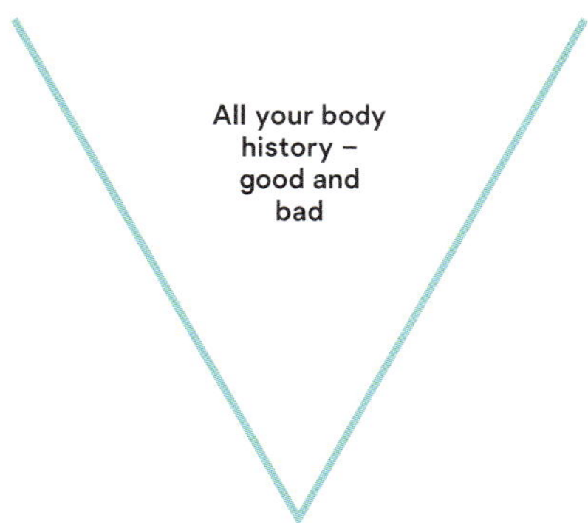

You could use our model here to look at yourself and your exercise history, from an internal process perspective. Get some ideas down about what preconceptions you have about your body and exercise. Note what kind of relationship you have with your body. Then look at how you would like to develop. Remember, self-acceptance is about accepting all your potential, as well as your limitations! Our relationship with our bodies lies somewhere in between these two concepts.

We also have a preliminary questionnaire to get you started. We encourage you to note down your answers and to revisit this from time to time. We hope this gentle directive thinking will help you on this new journey with your body.

Body questionnaire

Philosophy

- What is your philosophy in life for your body?

▶ What things did your parents teach you about your body, and how to look after it?

▶ What were your favourite physical activities with your body when you were growing up?

- What messages have you received about your body's potential, your body's drawbacks, and what type of a body it is?

- Are there any important things that happened to you physically that hindered or enhanced your physical development?

Feelings and emotional life

- How does your body react to stress?

- What makes your body relax?

- Where do you feel things in your body?

Your body and sexuality

- How do you feel about your body?

- Is your body a source of pleasure or discomfort?

Purpose

- What are your hopes for engaging with your body via this book?

- What would you like your relationship with your body to be like?

- What makes your body feel great?

Use this space to add any additional notes

Section

Applying 123 to individual muscles

In this section we will focus on one area of the body and offer you three exercises for that area: 1 strength, 2 stretch and 3 release. We have chosen three areas of the body to represent the three ways you can use this triangle model. It is important for us, at this point, to let you know that our triangle model is flexible, in that the order of strength, stretch, release can be played around with. Here is our model developed to indicate this point.

Rotatable triangle model

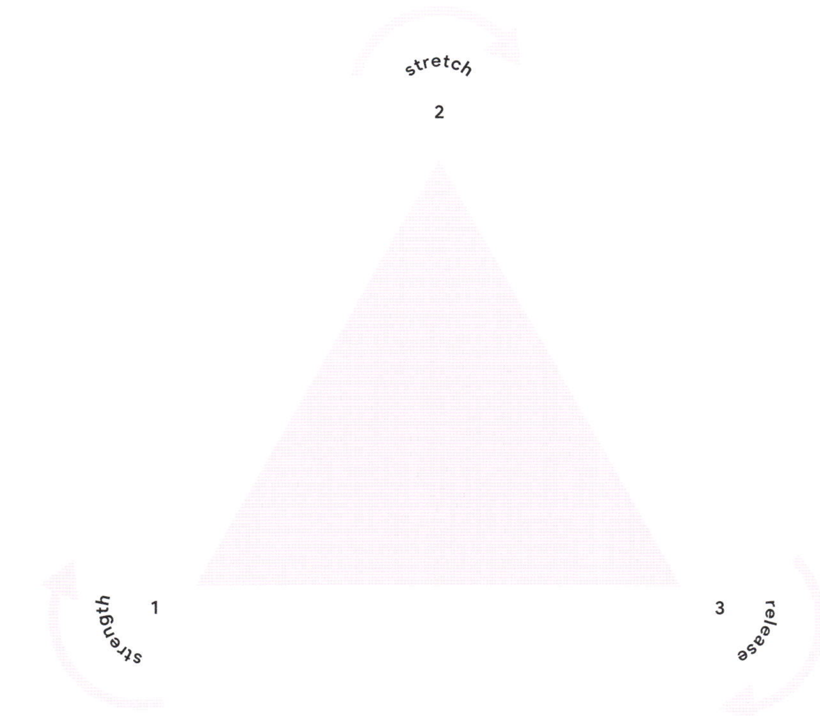

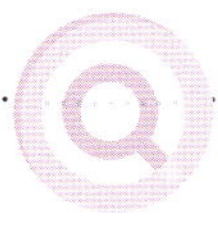

Spotlight: Sides of the waist

You can adapt this information for any area of the body, but we will start with the sides of the waist. Professional dancers use the waist muscles to achieve several movements. They might need waist muscles to help stabilise the pelvis or maintain a length in their sides when lifting one of their legs, or they may need to maintain an aligned position whilst being held aloft in the air. The sides of the waist are often neglected in conditioning programmes. These areas contribute to hip and shoulder stability, as well as good back health. For your everyday person, we might need to maintain effective waist muscles to keep a length through the body whilst swimming or to maintain an erect spine when carrying shopping back from the supermarket. Either way, it is a good idea to have a strategy to strengthen, stretch and release this area. The following exercises show some options for doing just that!

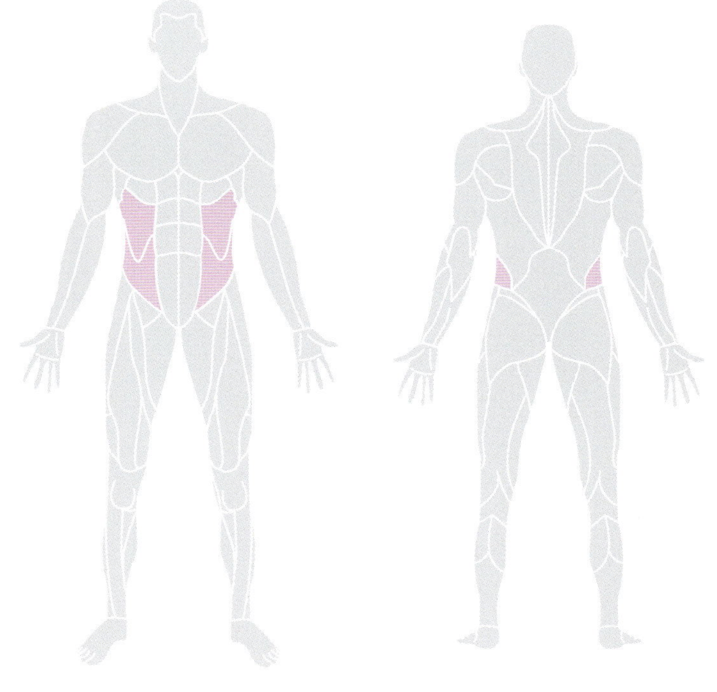

SIDE LEG LIFT (STRENGTH)

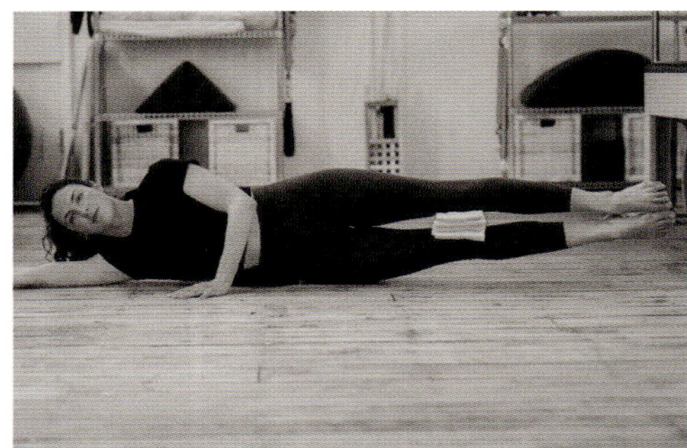

Purpose: To work the obliques and generally the side body.

Prepare: Lie on your side, resting your head on your lower outstretched arm. Rest your top hand just in front of your chest to balance. Draw your belly in and squeeze your inner thighs together, placing a block between your knees. Draw the shoulder blade of your top arm down and elongate throughout the body.

Perform: Lift up your legs whilst holding your inner thighs together with the block and then lower back down again.

Prudence: Keep your feet slightly in front of your body. Lift your legs to the point of aligning them with your body.

INTENSE SIDE STRETCH

Purpose: To stretch the sides and waist.

Prepare: Position your bent leg knee comfortably as shown. Vertically elongate your spine as you inhale. Reach the same arm as the bent leg to the ceiling. Keep your other arm on the floor with your palm facing up.

Perform: Reach up and over your straight leg and keep your chest facing forward.

Prudence: Keep a lift in your waist to avoid pinching your back or spine on the side you are leaning towards.

LOWER BACK RELEASE VAR. NO. 1

Purpose: To release the lower region of the back – this area can tighten and overwork if your side body isn't in good condition.

Prepare: Draw in your stomach and tuck your pelvis slightly, imprinting your back into a release ball.

Perform: Rotate your knees towards the direction of the side that the ball is on and back again. Repeat this back and forth 10 times. Move the ball 1cm down the lower back and repeat. Continue down your spine until you reach the pelvis.

Prudence: Stay off any bones, especially your spine.

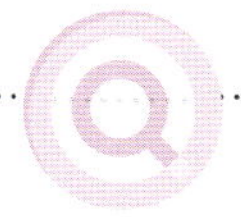

Spotlight: Buttock muscles

Let us have a look at applying the 123 Approach to another specific muscle. The buttock muscles (nicknamed the glutes) are a good place to go next as they are the largest muscles in the human body. The buttock muscles are made up of four muscles that all control different movements. However, we are going to look at how they contribute to a sit-to-stand movement. When getting up from sitting to standing or walking, they are the powerhouse that propel us forward. As stated earlier, although our 123 Approach is structured, it is not rigid. To elaborate, we mean that you do not have to first strengthen, then secondly stretch and third release.

Here, we feel that when stretching these large muscles they benefit from first being released. So, in this example we will **1 strength, 2 release and then 3 stretch**. Of course, this may not be the best for everyone, but we hope you will experiment and discover what works for you. In fact, that will be a theme throughout this book: we will continue to encourage you to connect with, and develop a relationship with, your body.

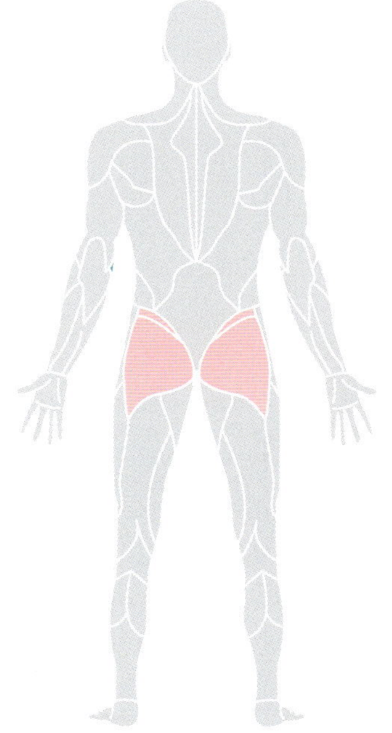

We have you on all fours in the exercise that follows to stabilise your pelvis and lower back. With the other leg on the floor, it helps keep the pelvis in a neutral position, which is aided by keeping your stomach in and aiming for a length in your lower back.

BUTTOCK MUSCLES PULSES (STRENGTH)

Purpose: To strengthen the buttock muscles.

Prepare: On all fours, make sure your hands are underneath the shoulders and your knees are underneath the hips. Gently draw in the stomach to maintain a neutral spine.

Perform: Lift one leg, keeping the angle of the knee at 90 degrees. Pulse the heel up and down to work into the buttock muscles.

Prudence: Keep the shoulder blades gently drawing down the back. Maintain a neutral spine and manage how high the leg lift is based on this position.

BUTTOCK MUSCLES RELEASE VAR. NO. 1

Purpose: To release the buttock muscles.

Prepare: Lie on your back with your knees bent and place a release ball on the upper part of the buttock muscles.

Perform: Drop the knee out to the side on the side that the ball is on.

Prudence: Remain on the muscles, not the bones or joints.

BUTTOCK MUSCLES STRETCH

Purpose: To stretch the back and the outside of the hips.

Prepare: Lie in a constructive rest position.

Perform: Cross your ankle over the knee. Raise the legs towards the chest. Briefly lift your head and chest and take hold of the parallel thigh. Then lower the head and chest, keeping hold of the thigh. Pull your legs towards you.

Prudence: Maintain a neutral neck. Flex the foot for additional knee support.

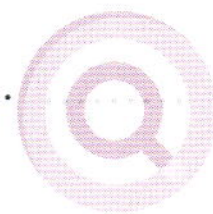

Spotlight: Outside front of hip and thigh

The external rotators of the hip offer us the opportunity to show why you might want to start with release work first. This front outside of hip muscle often becomes problematic when muscles in the back of the hip are weak. Release work and stretching can help to keep it from dominating. So, in this sequence of exercises we will **1 release, 2 strength and 3 stretch**. We use the release exercise first to loosen the side front aspect of the hip, which typically overworks in the execution of the exercise that follows, the Clam. By loosening this area first, it allows us to 'quieten' this muscle so we can optimise the correct gluteal muscle when targeting the area with the Clam exercise. The following pages show what these exercises look like together.

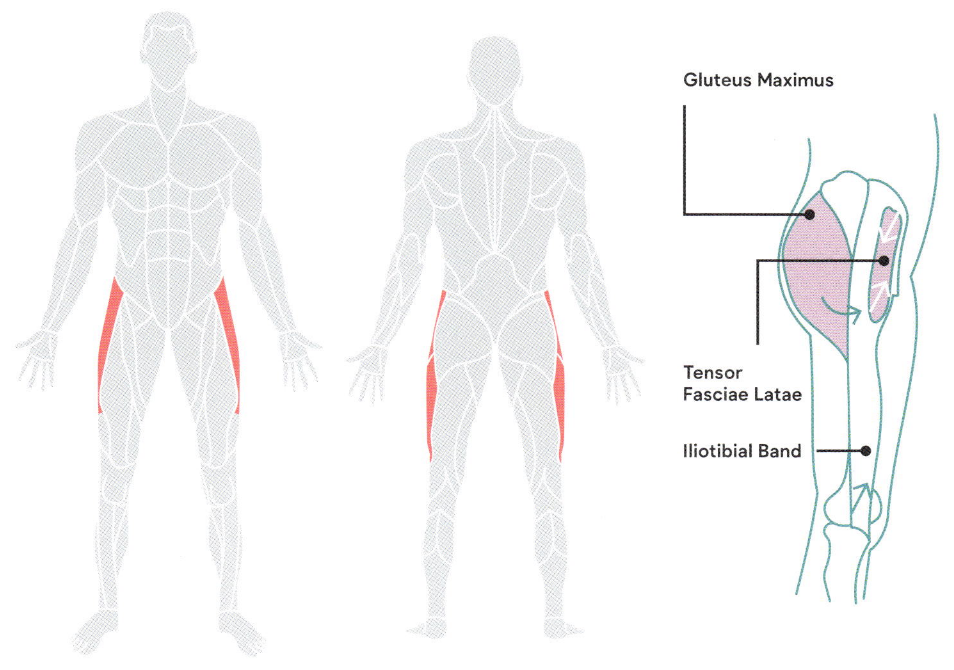

OUTSIDE OF HIP RELEASE VAR. NO. 1

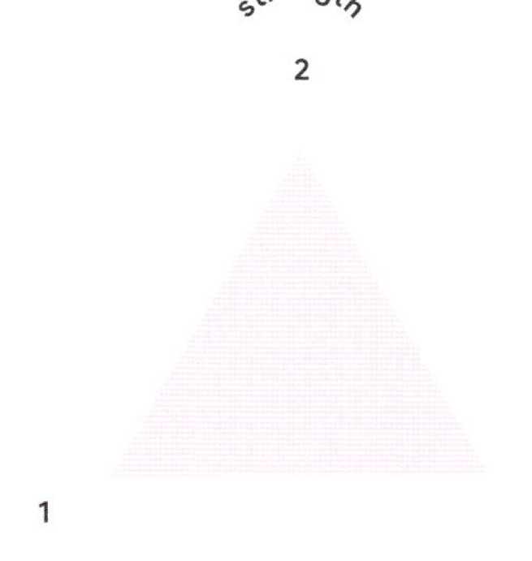

Purpose: To loosen the outside top of the thigh.

Prepare: Lie on your side with an arm stretched on the floor so your head can rest on it.

Perform: Place a release ball on the outside hip muscle located between the hip bone and the top of your thigh bone.

Prudence: Stay on the muscle, avoiding bones or joints.

CLAM (STRENGTH)

Purpose: To activate and work the lower glute muscles.

Prepare: Lie on one side with your head resting on the extended lower arm.

Perform: Activate the lower gluteal muscle. Imagine your thigh being pulled away from the hip joint. Open your knee just enough to work the lower glute. Squeeze your heels together as you do this.

Prudence: Aim to work specifically on the lower glute without over-relying on the hip flexor or outside of the hip muscle.

PIGEON VAR. NO. 1 (STRETCH)

Purpose: To stretch the back and sides of the hips.

Prepare: Assume the all fours position.

Perform: Place the left knee on the floor on the outside of the left hand and place the left foot on the floor close to the right hip, resulting in the outside of the left lower leg having contact with the floor. Slide the right leg back and away from your hands on the floor to lower the thigh of the right leg towards the floor.

Prudence: If you experience discomfort in the knee or lower back, choose another glute stretch that we have recommended (such as on pages 38 and 57). Try to keep the pelvis level with the floor.

In this section we have demonstrated three different orders to our 123 Approach, and reasoned why you might choose any of these strategies. Learning when and how to vary these orders will enable you to manage the tension in your body to optimal effect.

Section

WELCOME

Applying 123 to day-to-day movement

In **Section 1** we laid out how to apply the 123 Approach to an individual muscle. Essentially, how to strength, stretch and release it. The benefits of spending time each day doing this include:

- Activating the muscle for use, rather than letting it lie dormant through bad habits.
- Maintaining its flexibility, so it doesn't begin to restrict movement.
- Keeping it tension free, so it does not develop weak points, which may be more likely to get injured.

In **Section 2**, we will lay out how to apply our 123 Approach to some day-to-day activities that most of us contend with. We have chosen three movements that link to our cardio activities. The three movements are **sit to stand**, **walking** and **reaching and rotating**.

In **Section 3**, we will relate sit to stand movements to **cycling**; we will relate walking to **running** in **Section 4**; and we will relate reaching and rotating to **swimming** in **Section 5**. This offers a clear development throughout this book that you can use immediately or use to progress onto at a later stage.

Firstly, we need to develop our model to prepare our thinking!

Warm-ups and cool-downs with PER

If you can learn to **(P)repare (E)xercise (R)ecover** with the 123 Approach to Fitness, your body will feel better than it has done in years!

In this section, we will take the 123 Approach a few steps further. We will demonstrate how to break down a movement into its component parts (see page 49). Additionally, we will show you how to combine breaking down a movement with applying our 123 Approach both pre- and post-exercise. Once you understand the basic principles behind this approach, you can apply them to any activity.

PER diagram

Here is a model we call our **PER diagram** to help with your thinking. As you can see, it lays out that you can use the 123 Approach before and after exercise as a way to prepare your body for movement and to help your body with recovery from movement.

Note that the numbers in this diagram are in different positions on each triangle. This indicates that we can use any combination of the three options (strength, stretch and release), depending on your chosen activity's conditioning needs, for recovery and in preparation for exercise.

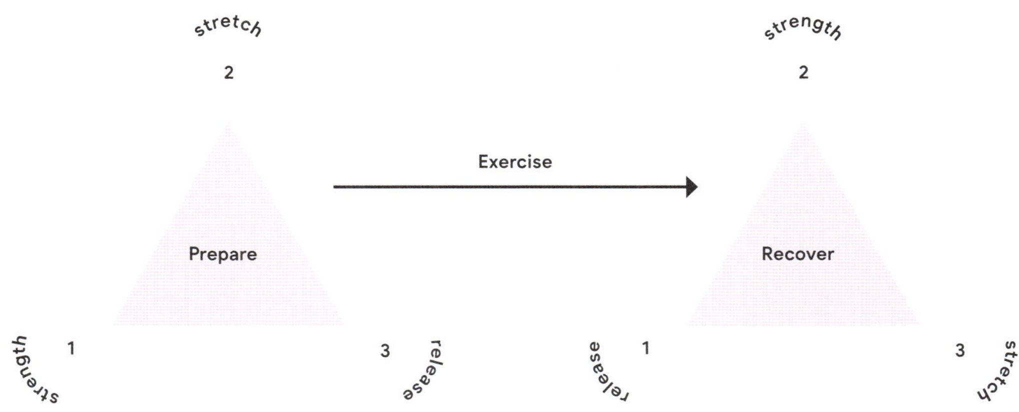

Day-to-day activities

Remember that your body has numerous muscles that work together to create movement. Here are three day-to-day movements that we are going to focus on. We chose these movements as we feel they cover most of the common movements that we go through each day. When considering an exercise programme to keep your body in good working order, we feel these will help you to keep limber, supple and relaxed!

- We all **sit to stand** numerous times in a day.
- We all **walk** somewhere at some point in a day.
- We all **reach** for something that we want regularly.
- We all **rotate** around to look when something, or someone, has caught our attention.

In this section we will break down these movements into phases. That will enable us to work on some specific elements to improve the overall movement patterns. Let's begin with the first one, sit to stand.

Preparing for sit to stand

So, let's look at this short programme of exercises that will help prepare your body for sit to stand movements. We will develop this later to show you how this relates to cycling as one option for your cardiovascular exercise. We will begin by breaking down the movement into its component parts:

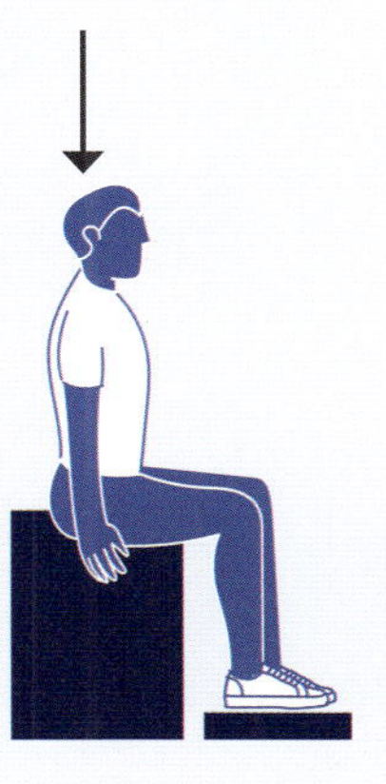

Start position

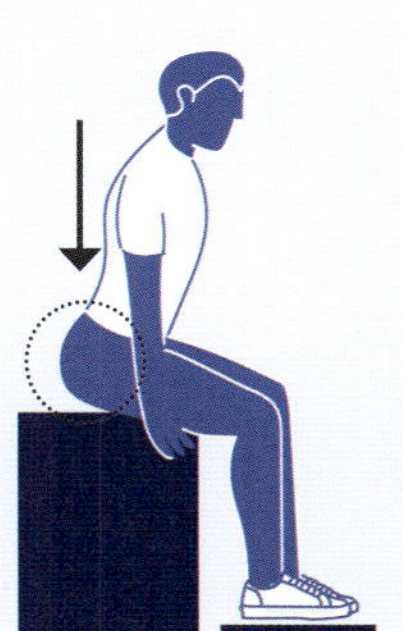

Phase 1:
Flexion moment
Hamstrings

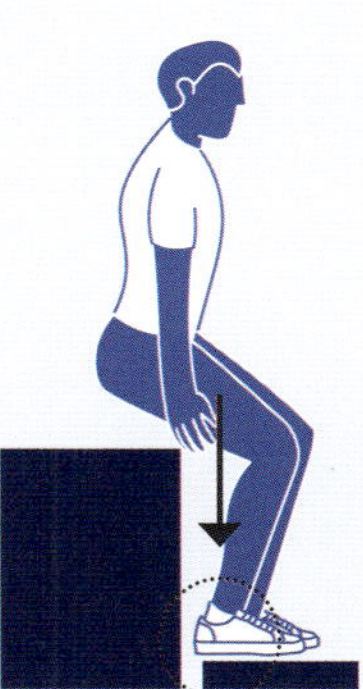

Phase 2:
Transfer moment
Buttocks

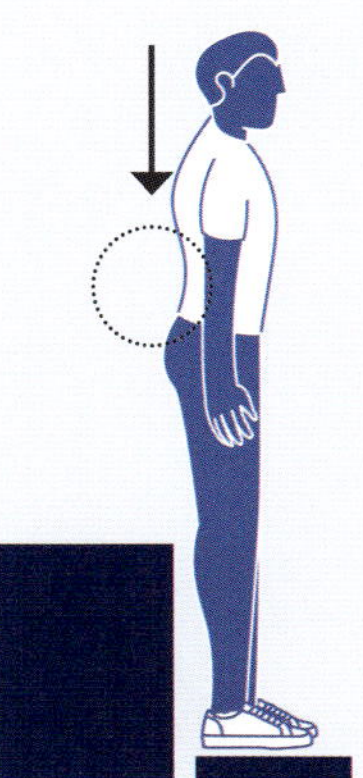

Phase 3:
Extension
Core and back

Phase 1: Hamstrings

The muscles involved in Phase 1 are the hamstrings. They need to lengthen for you to fold forward in the hips. If your hamstrings are tight, then your lower spine will be forced to curve forward to achieve this movement. This is known to be the cause of numerous appointments with physios for lower back pain. So, it's important to stretch your hamstrings.

STRETCHING YOUR HAMSTRINGS

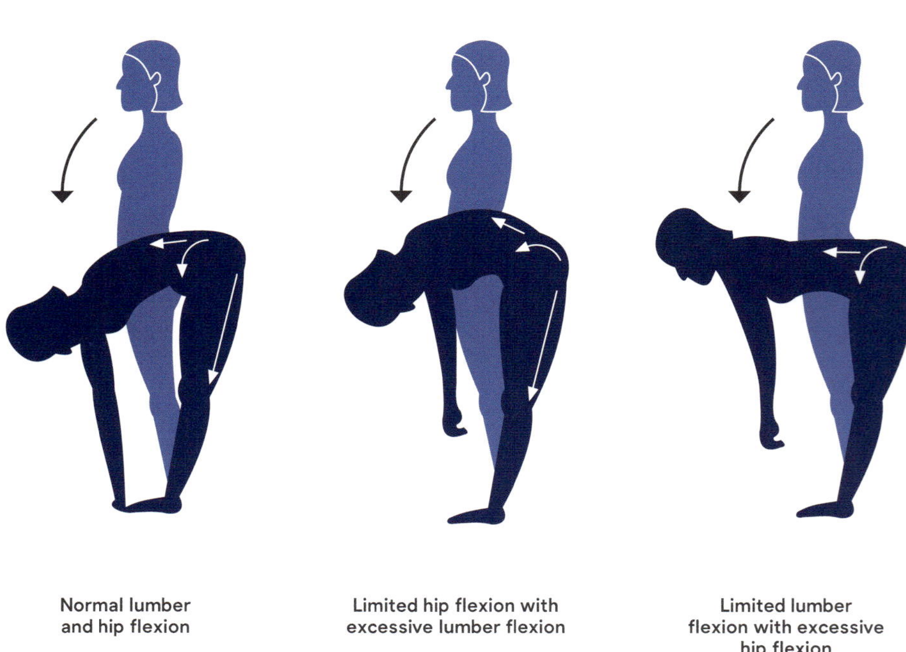

Normal lumber and hip flexion

Limited hip flexion with excessive lumber flexion

Limited lumber flexion with excessive hip flexion

However, to stretch any muscle we recommend first strengthening it to warm it up and to prepare it for being used. So, we would suggest **1 strengthen** the back of the thighs, **2 stretch** them out and **3 release** them. The following exercises show how you might do that.

BRIDGING VAR. NO. 1 (STRENGTH)

Purpose: To work the hamstrings.

Prepare: Lie in a constructive rest position with your feet on a horizontal roller.

Perform: Squeeze the lower glutes. Lift your pelvis until it is in line with your shoulders and knees. Extend one leg, then lower the hips back down. Finally, return the extended foot onto the roller. Alternate sides as you go through your repetitions.

Prudence: Maintain neutral spine. Keep your feet and knees in parallel.

BACK OF THIGH STRETCH VAR. NO. 1

Purpose: To stretch the back of the legs.

Prepare: Lie on your back with your legs straight and a strap within reach.

Perform: Raise your right leg and place the strap over the ball of the foot. Hold onto the ends of the strap with both hands. Extend the right leg up to the sky. Flex the foot.

Prudence: Keep the right hip on the floor and keep the spine neutral.

Spotlight: Lateral* back of thigh (Hamstring – Biceps Femoris)

We could go back and forth through this process of strengthening and stretching for weeks or months at a time, but eventually our back of thigh muscles will develop trigger points. This means that they can be more at risk of injury when stretching and strengthening and this is the point where you can become injured! Additionally, this muscle typically works more laterally than medially on most people. This can be observed in the feet turning out when completing a bridge, for example. The next exercise shows a way we can release our back of thigh. We would recommend paying particular attention to the lateral part of this muscle when releasing it.

* *Medial means closer to the midline of the body. Lateral means closer to the outside of the body.*

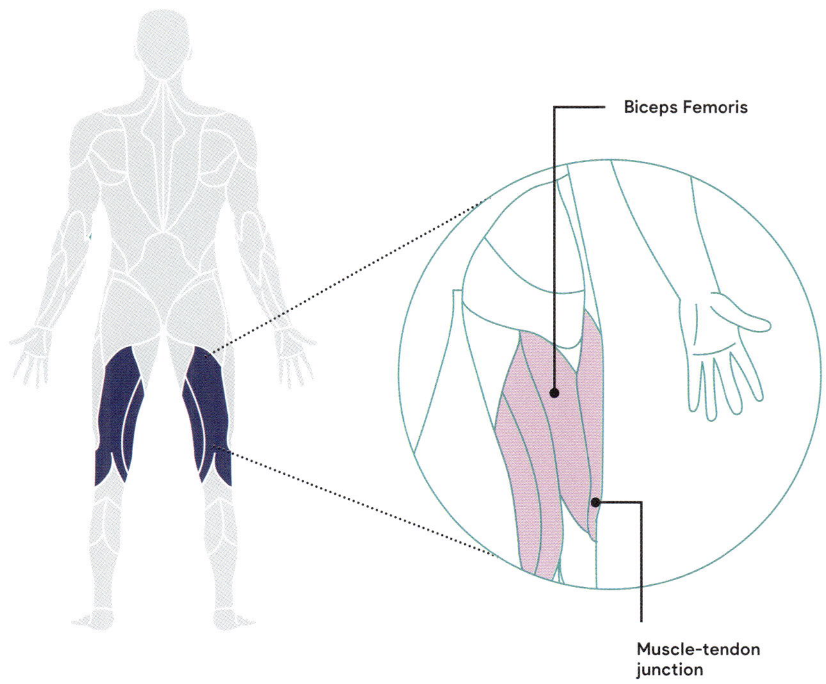

Stool
+
Release ball

BACK OF THIGH RELEASE VAR. NO. 1

Purpose: To release the lateral hamstrings.

Prepare: Sit on a stool or chair where the lower legs can dangle.

Perform: Place a release ball in the belly of the lateral back of your thigh, where indicated on page 53. Put your hands on your thigh and push down. Explore trigger points along the length of the muscle.

Prudence: Stay on muscle as it is a tubular shape and the ball can slide off it. Stay away from bone and joints.

Phase 2: Buttocks

In Phase 2 of the sit-to-stand movement, we use the buttock muscles to drive the hips forward into a standing position. It is particularly important to try to utilise the lower buttock muscles when going through this movement. At this point, we are looking for power and range of movement, which we will use **1 strength** and **2 stretch** to achieve.

Spotlight: Buttocks

The buttock muscles are the largest muscles in the body.

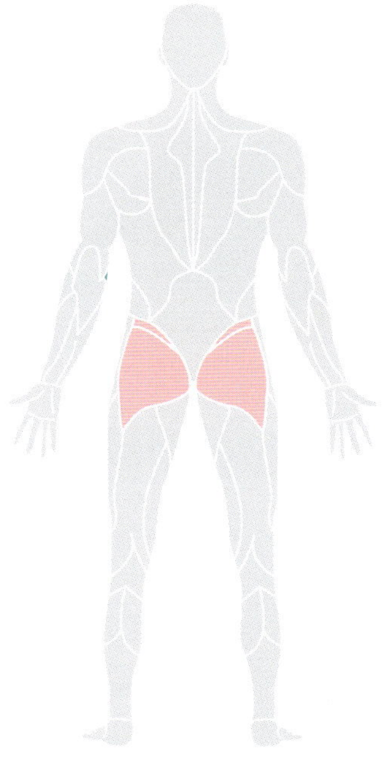

SINGLE LEG SIT TO STAND VAR. NO. 1 (STRENGTH)

Purpose: To improve the hip mobility, strengthen the buttocks and improve balance.

Prepare: Sit on the front edge of a stool or chair with your feet hip distance apart, spine neutral and shoulders relaxed. The knee angle of the working leg should be no more acute than 90 degrees. Hover the other leg off the floor slightly. Hold on to something if you need to.

Perform: Actively squeeze the lower part of your buttock muscles. Fold forward in the hips and once you feel you have enough of a tipping point, press the working foot into the floor to come up to standing.

Prudence: Keep your spine neutral and maintain the lower buttock activation throughout.

The buttock muscles can also play a part in restricting our ability to fold forward from the hips if they are tight. Here is an exercise to help with that:

Stool

SEATED BUTTOCK STRETCH VAR. NO. 1

Purpose: To stretch the buttock muscles and outer hips.

Prepare: Sit on a stool or chair towards the front edge with your knees and hips at 90 degrees.

Perform: Cross one ankle onto the opposite thigh just above the knee. Lift in the waist and lean the body forward, hinging from your hips. Rest your hands lightly on your lifted shin.

Prudence: Try to maintain a straight back. Be responsive to any knee pain and choose an alternative buttock stretch if problematic.

Here is how we can release the buttock muscles, as they have built tension during the single leg sit-to-stand movement on page 56, which can contribute to a tightness in the lower back area.

Release ball

BUTTOCK MUSCLES RELEASE VAR. NO. 2

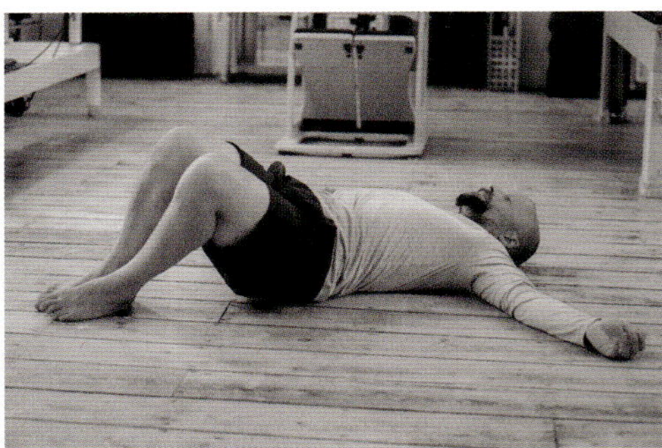

Purpose: To release the buttock muscles.

Prepare: Lie on your back with your knees bent and place a release ball on the upper part of the buttock muscles.

Perform: Drop both knees out to the side that the ball is on.

Prudence: Remain on the muscle, not bone or joints.

Phase 3: Core and back

In Phase 3, once upstanding, our core muscles and back extensors help us to maintain an upright position. For this to feel as effortless as possible, it is a good idea to keep these areas of the body in good condition. This section shows some exercises for that purpose.

Spotlight: Core and back extensors

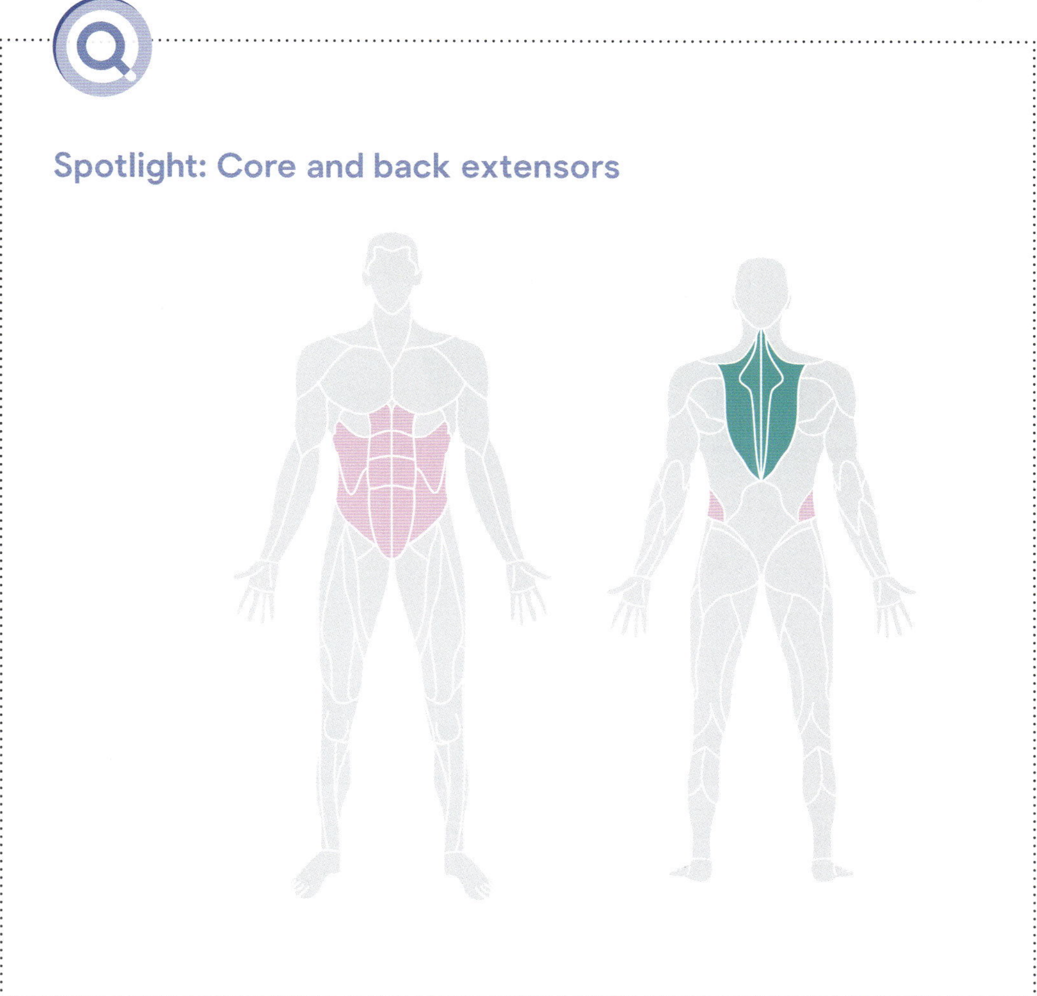

DEEP CORE (STRENGTH)

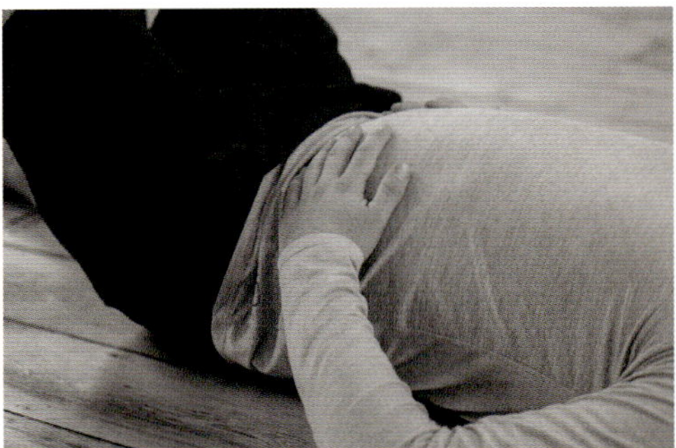

Purpose: To strengthen the deep abdominal muscles.

Prepare: Lie on your back with your knees bent and your hands just below your navel.

Perform: Breathe in and let your abdomen expand. Breathe out and pull the lower belly in towards the spine.

Prudence: Keep your legs parallel, shoulders and neck relaxed.

ARROW VAR. NO. 1 (STRENGTH)

Purpose: To strengthen the mid to upper back.

Prepare: Lie on your front with your arms down by your waist and palms facing up.

Perform: Lift the arms. Draw your shoulder blades down as you lift the head and chest off the floor. Lower the back down.

Prudence: Draw the stomach in gently to keep the lower back in neutral.

The core can take a lot of tension as it is made up of many smaller muscles that work together to distribute the load. The core exercises we have just done are particularly low level as well. We can therefore go straight to stretch and release work for the back.

CAT STRETCH VAR. NO. 1

Purpose: To stretch the back muscles and between the shoulder blades.

Prepare: Assume an all fours position with your wrists under your shoulders and your knees under your hips. Return to neutral and perform 10 repetitions.

Perform: Draw your tummy in and round the back as much as you can. Return to a neutral spine position.

Prudence: Maintain a length in the back of the neck at all times. Tuck the toes under if your feet start to cramp.

MID-BACK RELEASE

2 release balls

Purpose: To release the mid-back muscles (otherwise known as the thoracic region of the back).

Prepare: Lie in a constructive rest position. Place release balls on either side of your spine, just below your shoulder blades.

Perform: Take 10 deep breaths. Move 1cm down the mid-back and repeat. Continue down your spine until you reach the lower ribs.

Prudence: Stay off any bones, especially your spine.

In summary, this can be a low-level routine to perform every day to help maintain good back health and continued functional movement when sitting to standing. Breaking down the sit to stand movement into its component parts allows you to explore the body in a more thorough and detailed way. This can help with squat movements in the gym as well as day-to-day tasks like lifting objects from the floor. We will demonstrate later in Section 3 how this can also lead on to cycling.

Preparing for walking

Continuing along the lines of using 1 2 3 like ingredients, we will now look at a short programme of exercises to help with walking. Keep in mind that these are exercises to help proactively manage tension in your body that develops in relation to walking. We will also develop this movement and programme and show how it relates to running. As before, we will begin by breaking down the movement into its component parts.

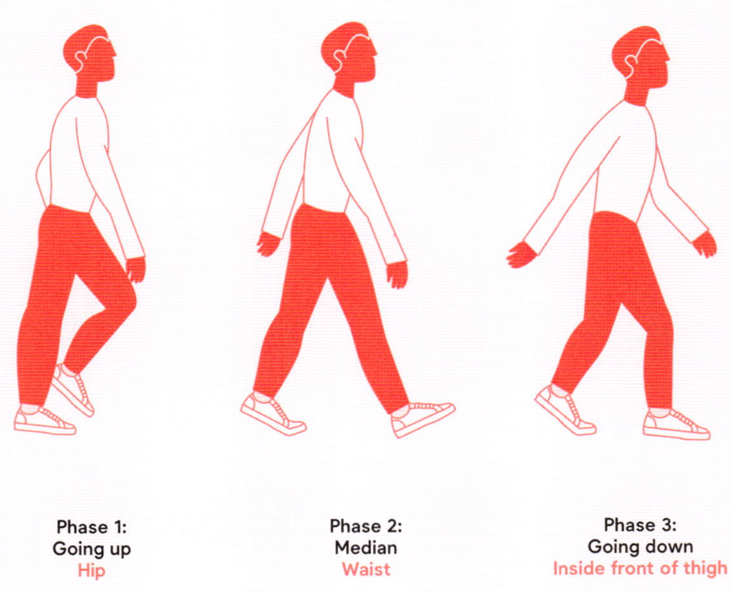

Phase 1: Hip

If we look at Phase 1: Going up of this movement to begin with, our first step involves lifting the leg. The muscles in the front of our hip perform the movement of lifting our leg to take a first step. The following exercises show how we could make that muscle activation conscious.

KNEE FLOATS VAR. NO. 1 (STRENGTH)

Purpose: To strengthen the hip flexors.

Prepare: Lie on your back with your knees bent, legs parallel.

Perform: Raise one leg slowly, bringing the knee above the hip. Draw the stomach in as you do this. Release the stomach when lowering the leg back down. Alternate legs as you go through your repetitions.

Prudence: Keep the pelvis and spine neutral and the upper body relaxed.

We also push off the back leg and press the floor behind us in tandem with lifting the front leg. Here is an exercise to mimic that movement:

PLANK WITH LEG LIFT (STRENGTH)

Purpose: Full body strengthening with a strong focus on the arms and core.

Prepare: On all fours, place your shoulders over your wrists and your hips above your knees.

Perform: Step your legs back one at a time into a plank position. Lengthen through the arms and slightly draw the tummy in. Lift one leg off the floor, being sure to keep the pelvis level and the spine neutral. Place the foot back on the floor.

Prudence: Keep a light engagement of the abdominal muscles to maintain a neutral lower back.

We also press off the back foot, working the muscles in the calf to help propel us forward. Here is an exercise for this:

HEEL RAISES VAR. NO. 1 (STRENGTH)

Purpose: To strengthen the lower legs.

Prepare: Stand with your feet hip distance apart.

Perform: Press down into the balls of the feet and slowly raise the heels, then control the heels back down.

Prudence: Distribute the weight evenly between the right and left feet.

We also use our postural back muscles to keep us upright, which can be supported with this exercise:

ARROW VAR. NO. 2 (STRENGTH)

Purpose: To strengthen the upper back.

Prepare: Lie down on the stomach and place the hands on the floor besides the hips, with the palms facing upwards.

Perform: Lift your arms, head and shoulders off the floor as you draw your shoulder blades down your back. Skim the floor with your fingertips as you take your arms out to a T-position. Bring your arms back to the waist. Lower your back down and repeat.

Prudence: Keep the back of the neck long by looking directly at the floor beneath your eyes.

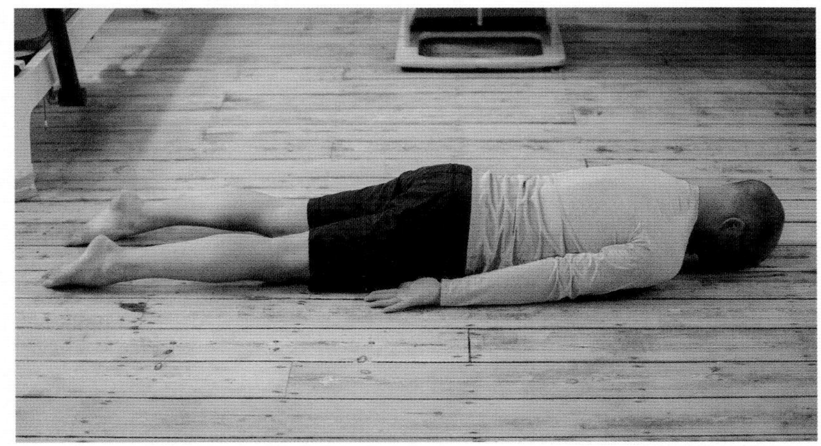

Arrow var. no. 2 (Strength)

Phase 2: Waist

As we step onto the front leg in Phase 2: Median, we use the rotational muscles in our waist (obliques) to counterbalance our bodies. This enables us to remain upright and not fall over. The following exercises will help with that:

Spotlight: Sides of the waist (Obliques) and Hip flexor (Psoas)

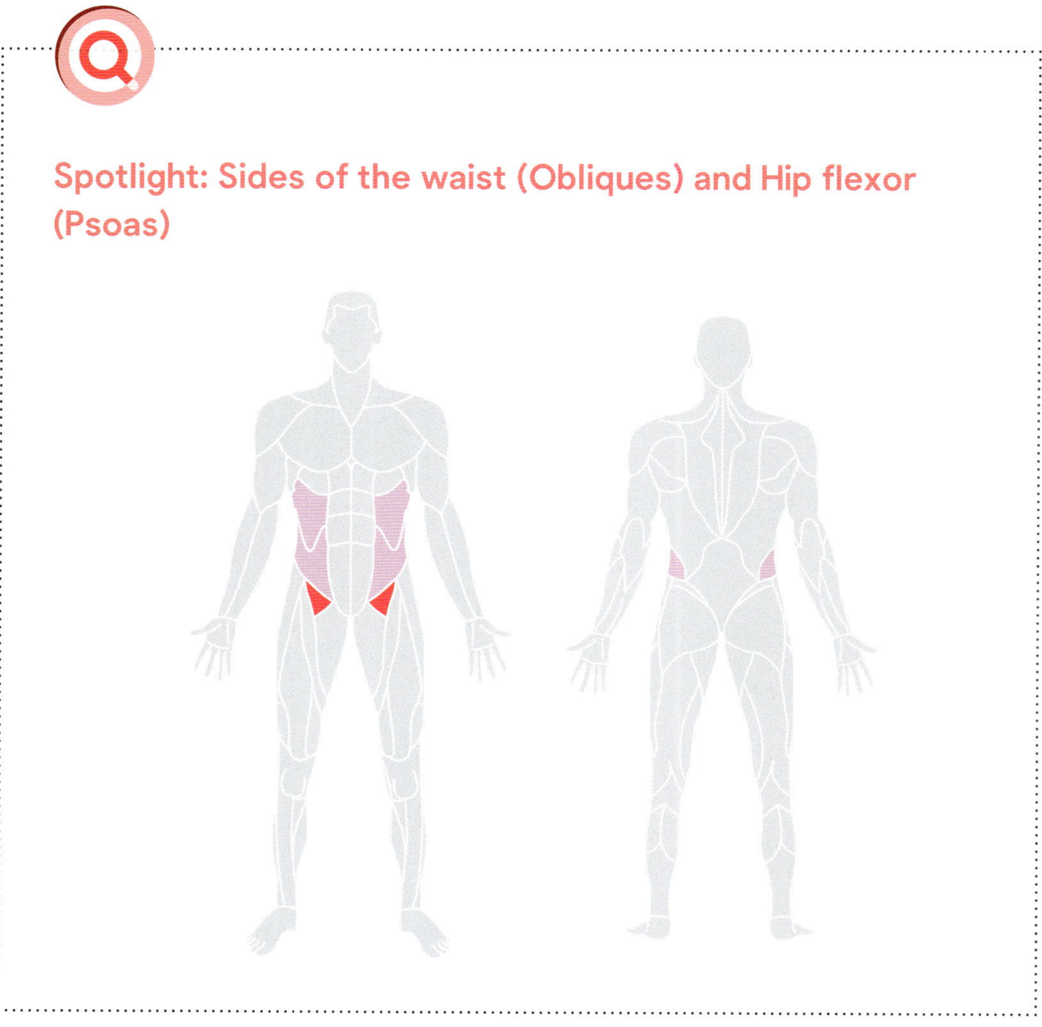

SEATED ROTATIONS (STRETCH)

Purpose: To mobilise the mid-spine and increase the suppleness of the back muscles.

Prepare: Sit upright on a chair or stool with your knees stacked above your ankles. Bring your arms up as if you are hugging a large ball in front of the chest. Alternate sides as you go through your repetitions.

Perform: Rotate the ribs, chest and head from side to side, as if looking over your shoulders.

Prudence: Keep the pelvis facing forwards and the legs still.

We might also stretch the front of the hip of the back leg to take a sizeable step. This area can pull on the lower back and cause discomfort there if it's too tight.

LOW LUNGE VAR. NO. 1 (STRETCH)

Purpose: To stretch the front of the hip.

Prepare: Assume an all fours position.

Perform: From kneeling, step one foot forward as far as you can into a deep lunge and place your hands on your front thigh.

Prudence: Keep the knee of your front leg directly over the heel of your front foot.

Spotlight: How the hip flexors influence the lower back

The deep muscles at the front of the hip are responsible for lifting the thigh when standing. If you are sitting a lot during the day or lifting the thighs repetitively, as in a running movement, these can tighten up. When these muscles do tighten, they pull on their attachment points, which are along the front of the lower spine. When this happens, it can lead to lower back pain. That is why it is important to keep this area stretched out.

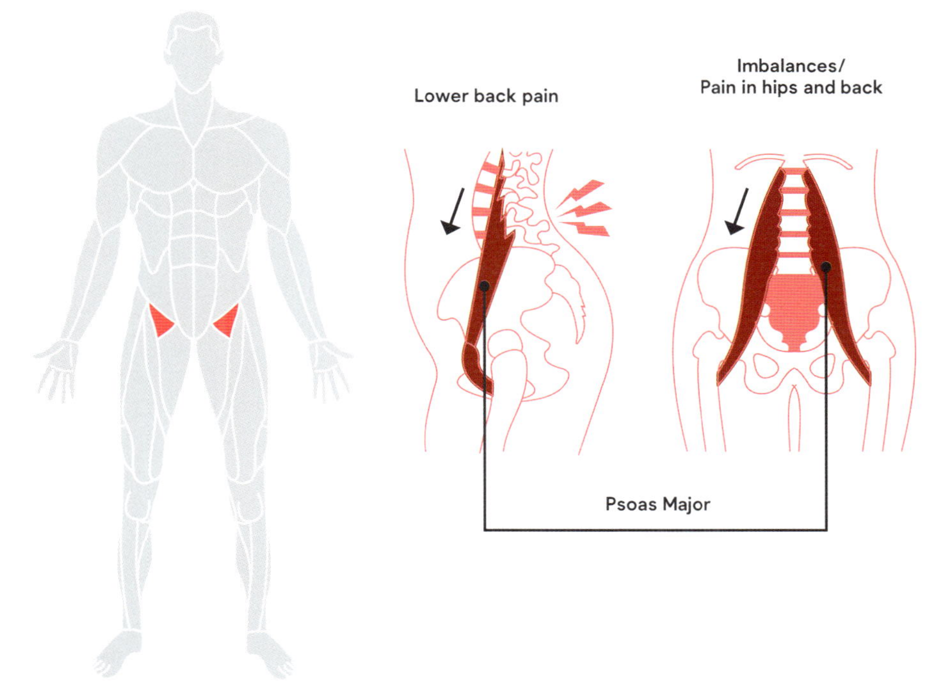

DEEP HIP FLEXOR RELEASE VAR. NO. 1

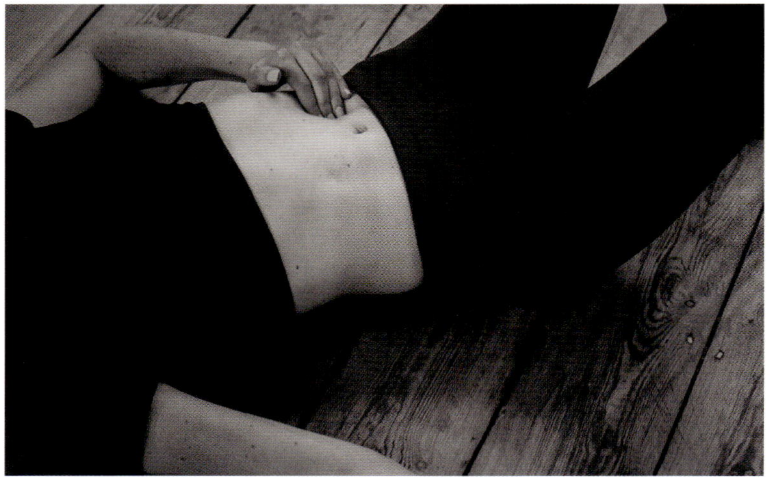

Purpose: To release the hip flexor.

Prepare: Lie in a constructive rest position and place your hands on the waist either side of the navel. In this first variation, float one leg up into tabletop whilst pressing into the waist. This should enable you to feel where the hip flexor is, as it will contract when you lift your knee.

Perform: Press into the waist on one side with the same side hand and pull out away from the navel.

Prudence: Aim to do this with an empty stomach.

Phase 3: Inside thigh

To keep the muscles of the front of the thigh in balance in Phase 3: Going down, it is important to condition them to activate on the inside of the thigh. If we don't address this area, we can overwork the muscles on the outside front of the thigh, which can lead to poor tracking of the kneecap and general knee discomfort. The following exercises can help with that.

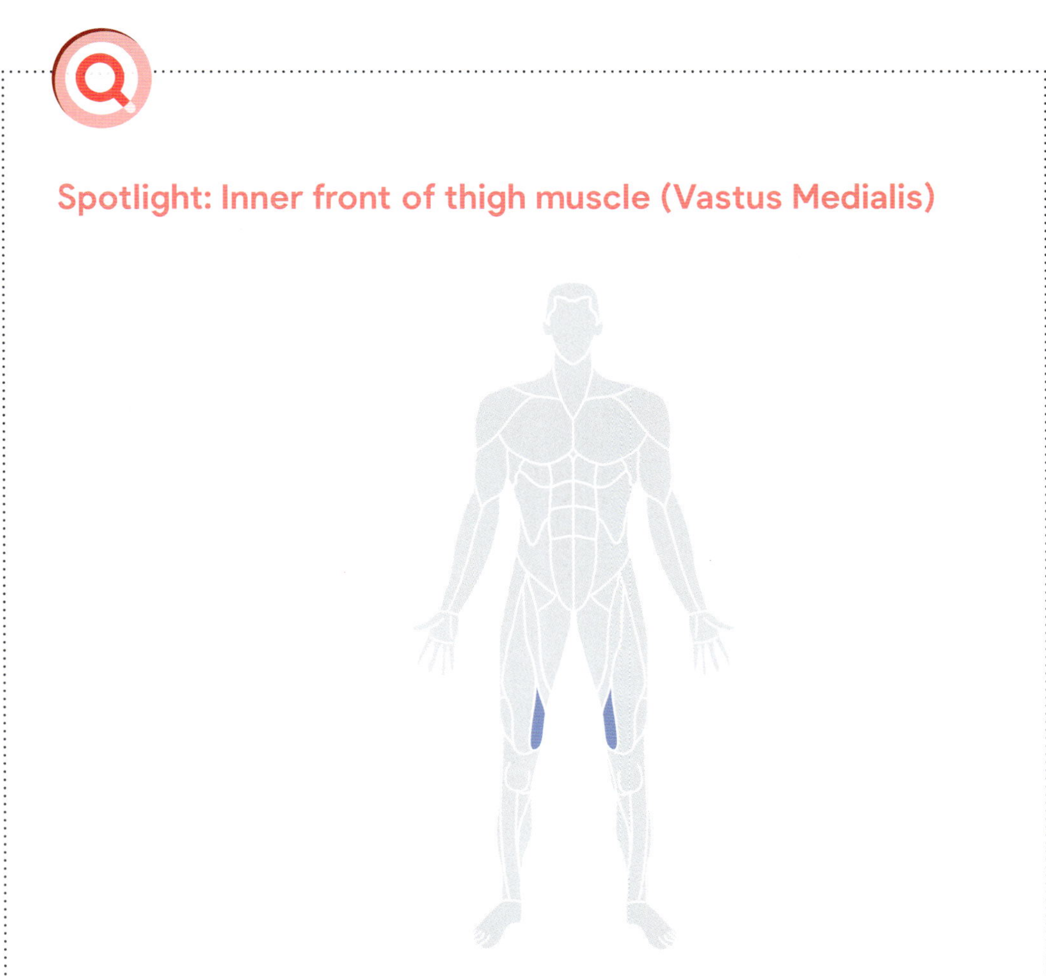

Spotlight: Inner front of thigh muscle (Vastus Medialis)

INSIDE FRONT OF THIGH VAR. NO. 1 (STRENGTH)

Purpose: To strengthen the innermost front of the thigh muscle.

Prepare: Lie on your back with a roller underneath the back of the thigh.

Perform: Straighten one leg. Flex your foot, point the foot and lower the foot back down.

Prudence: Make sure when you straighten your leg that you draw up the inner quad muscle and feel it tense. You can check this by feeling the muscle with your hand.

When we press off the leg after going down again, we have a slightly bent knee. This means the lower calf muscle works, rather than the upper calf muscle, which works when pushing off and the leg is straight, as in the Going up movement. Try this:

BENT LEG HEEL RAISES VAR. NO. 1 (STRENGTH)

Purpose: To strengthen the deep lower leg muscles.

Prepare: Stand with your feet hip distance apart and knees slightly bent.

Perform: Lift your heels off the floor as high as you can, resulting in the whole body lifting. Lower your heels back down.

Prudence: Keep the weight of the body slightly forward.

In this section we have shown you how to find, and activate, your muscles for walking. This simple programme will keep you in good shape when partaking in this simple cardiovasular activity.

Now you have prepared your body, you can enjoy a walk tension free, with a spring in your step!

Go for a walk

Recovering

We have all felt stiffness in our bodies after walking a lot. This will lead to some of the larger muscles needing to be stretch out, but also some smaller, harder to reach muscles that will need to be released off. The following sequence shows some exercises to help address the tension that has built up.

BUTTOCK MUSCLES RELEASE VAR. NO. 3

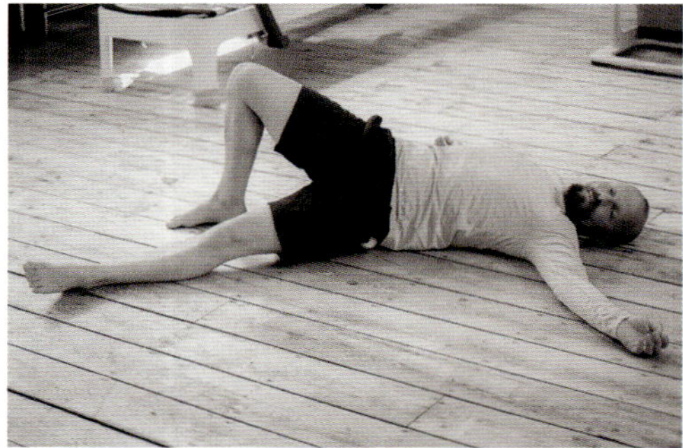

Purpose: To release the buttock muscles.

Prepare: Lie on your back with one leg stretched out along the floor, and the other leg bent with your foot resting on the floor.

Perform: Rotate in the direction of the straight leg and explore the different tight areas in the buttock muscles.

Prudence: Remain on the muscle, not bone or joints.

Release ball + platform

LOWER LEG RELEASE

Purpose: To release the deep lower leg muscles.

Prepare: You can use anything as a platform, but we recommend stacking a pile of 3 or 4 books with a release ball on top.

Perform: Sit on the floor and place one lower leg on the ball. Rest it there briefly, and then move it to a different spot on the lower leg.

Prudence: Keep the ball below the main bulk of the calf and above the Achilles.

LOWER BACK RELEASE VAR. NO. 2

Purpose: To release the lower region of the back – this area can tighten and overwork if your side body isn't in good condition.

Prepare: Lie in a constructive rest position. Place 2 release balls, one either side of the spine, just below the lower ribs.

Perform: Take 10 deep breaths. Move the balls 1cm down the lower back and repeat. Continue down the spine until reaching the pelvis.

Prudence: Stay off any bones, especially the spine.

ROTATIONAL HIP STRETCH VAR. NO. 1

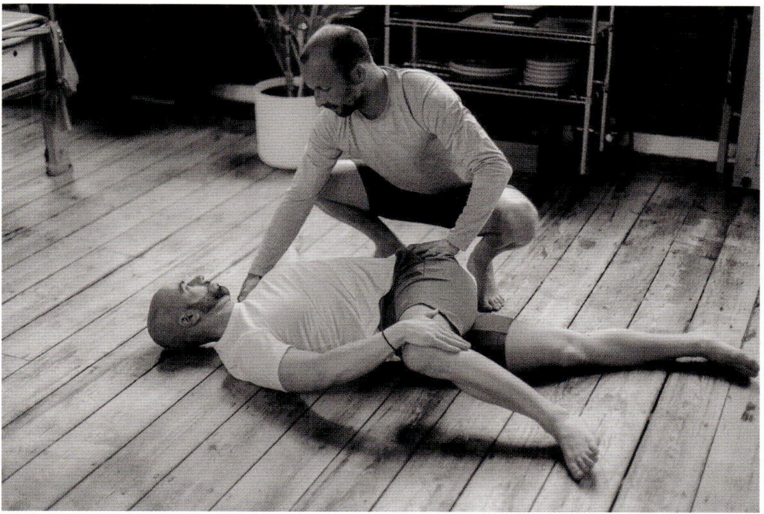

Purpose: To stretch the rotational lower back and the buttock muscles.

Prepare: Lie on the floor with your legs straight.

Perform: Raise one leg into tabletop position and rotate it across the body, encouraging it towards the floor with the opposite hand. Release the body back to the centre and bring the spine, leg and pelvis back to neutral. Alternate sides as you go through your repetitions.

Prudence: Position your head in a way that feels comfortable and allows your neck to relax. You can let it roll to either side as you take the twist.

CHILD'S POSE VAR. NO. 1 (STRETCH)

Purpose: To stretch the back and encourage relaxation.

Prepare: Assume an all fours position with toes untucked.

Perform: Sit your buttocks back onto the heels, folding at the hips with your forehead on the floor and arms resting out in front of you.

Prudence: Let the weight of the hips and head release.

PYRAMID POSE (STRETCH)

Purpose: To stretch the hamstrings.

Prepare: Stand with one leg in front of the other, with the front leg facing forwards and the back leg turned slightly out (about 45 degrees). Place hands on hips to keep the hips facing forwards and elongate both sides of the waist.

Perform: Fold forwards in the hips and relax the body over the front thigh. Place the fingertips of each hand on the floor on either side of the front foot. Soften the chest to the foot and then relax the back of the neck, allowing the forehead to reach in the direction of your shin. To come out of the stretch, deeply bend the front knee and return to standing.

Prudence: Allow the front knee to bend slightly to reduce the intensity.

LEG SLIDES (STRENGTH)

Purpose: To strengthen the deep core muscles.

Prepare: Lie down with one leg straight and one knee bent, hands on the lower tummy.

Perform: Breathe in to expand the abdomen. Slowly breathe out, pull the tummy in and bend the extended leg, sliding the foot parallel with the other leg. Breathe in to stretch the leg out again. Alternate the legs as you go through your repetitions.

Prudence: Keep the spine and pelvis neutral.

All these exercises are designed to release the tension in the back of our thighs, buttocks, lower back and calves. These are the areas that will predominantly tighten when walking a lot.

To summarise, we have used a combination of 1 strength, 2 stretch, 3 release when preparing for walking, with an emphasis on 1 strength. We then used a combination of 1 strength, 2 stretch and 3 release when dealing with the tension built up during walking, with an emphasis on 2 stretch and 3 release.

Leg slides (Strength)

Preparing for reaching and rotating

Finally, here we will look at reaching and rotating. We have combined these two movements together as they are often linked. We will also develop this movement and set of exercises by linking it to swimming later in the book.

Reaching and rotating movements use far less sizeable muscles than walking or sit to stand movements. As such, we might not need the same level of recovery from this. We now take you back to where we started with our model, in its simplest form:

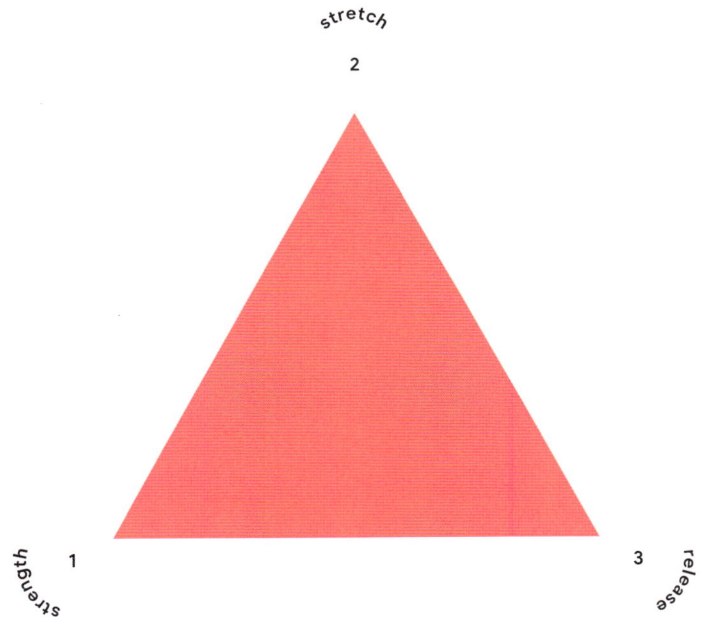

This routine will go through **1 strength, 2 stretch** and **3 release** exercises designed to keep your body in good condition for reaching and rotating. We will move on from this in the following sections to show you how our 123 model can be used to various effect, depending on what activity you are doing.

If we are reaching for something overhead, this can involve a transfer of weight onto one leg. This involves heightened balance. One of the causes of many admissions each year to the NHS are falls, so balance is a good thing to be working on regularly. We thought we would start with balance here.

Reach and rotate
Obliques, shoulders, glutes

TREE POSE (STRENGTH)

Purpose: To strengthen the legs and improve balance.

Prepare: Stand with your feet hip distance apart.

Perform: Bring your weight onto one leg whilst slightly squeezing the lower buttock of that leg. Place the sole of the other foot against the inside of the opposite thigh, encouraging the knee of the lifted leg to face out to the side. Press the foot and thigh in towards each other. Place the hands together in a prayer position in front of the chest.

Prudence: Keep a steady focus on something that is not moving. Keep the pelvis facing forwards.

Tree pose (Strength)

We also rotate when we reach. It is important to keep the muscles in the waist active and strong for this movement.

OBLIQUE CURLS VAR. NO. 1 (STRENGTH)

Purpose: To strengthen the obliques.

Prepare: Assume a constructive rest position and place your hands behind your head.

Perform: Pull the lower tummy in as you lift the head and shoulders and rotate your upper body in one direction. Then lower back down to neutral. Alternate sides as you go through your repetitions.

Prudence: Bring both shoulder blades off the floor when you lift. Maintain a relaxed neck.

Spotlight: Improving posture and reducing tension

Some people only think of the biceps and triceps when thinking of arm work. We like to think about the arms being connected into the back. This is how arms are used in dance. Thinking about a back connection when using your arms can aid good posture and functional shoulder movements.

Several things can contribute to shoulder tension. Bad posture, muscle imbalance and overuse of the arms are all culprits to name a few. It is important to combine strategies when dealing with this issue. One way to help is to release the upper shoulders (as described on page 99). Another way is to address your posture (as described on page 68). Here we show you how to look at balancing the muscles below the shoulders with the muscles above the shoulders. Through combining these release and strengthening strategies with some stretching (as described on pages 33, 62 and 71), we would bet money that your shoulders will feel a whole lot better for it!

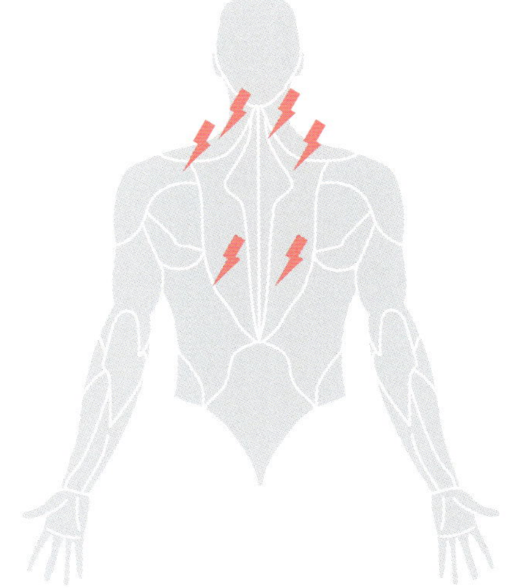

Here are two good exercises for improving posture and reducing tension:

OVERHEAD BACK MUSCLE PULLS (STRENGTH)

Purpose: To strengthen the areas below the shoulder blades and to improve the shoulder blade connection to the back.

Prepare: Wrap the TheraBand around an immovable surface. Lie on your back with your arms overhead on the floor, taking hold of the ends of the TheraBand. Make sure your arms are straight to begin with and that you have positioned yourself far enough away from the fixed point to have a little bit of tension in the band.

Perform: Draw your tummy in gently. Pull your hands down towards the waist, feeling the back work.

Prudence: Keep your lower spine in neutral. Your hands should be lifted 10cm off the floor throughout the movement.

KNEELING COBRA PRESS (STRETCH)

Purpose: To strengthen the front of the chest and the shoulders.

Prepare: Lie on your stomach with your hands under your shoulders.

Perform: Press away from the floor by straightening the arms. Lift the waist and draw the tummy in but keep the knees on the floor. Bend to return.

Prudence: Encourage your shoulder blades down your back to avoid neck tension.

When 'keeping the shoulders connected to the back,' as we say, the areas in the sides of the body can tighten up. A good way to take care of that tension, to loosen the front of the hip and open the side of the waist is this exercise:

KNEELING FRONT OF HIPS STRETCH

Purpose: To stretch the hip flexors.

Prepare: Assume an all fours position.

Perform: Step forward into a lunge position, placing the front knee directly over the heel. Keep your body in an upright position and place your hands onto the front thigh.

Prudence: Try to combine lifting in the waist whilst relaxing your shoulders.

With high usage of your arms, tension can build up in the shoulders and upper torso. We advise combining these areas when thinking about arm work *and* when releasing and stretching too. The following exercises release tension in these areas:

BACK OF SHOULDER STRETCH

Purpose: To stretch the back of the shoulders.

Prepare: Stand or sit with the spine neutral.

Perform: Bring one arm across the chest and take hold of your forearm with the opposite hand. Use your hand to pull the arm towards your chest and to bring it a little further across your body.

Prudence: Encourage your shoulder to drop away from your ear. Maintain a relaxed neck.

EAGLE ARMS VAR. NO. 1 (STRETCH)

Purpose: To stretch the back of the shoulders.

Prepare: Sit on a chair or stool or stand comfortably.

Perform: Cross one elbow on top of the other. With the hand of the underneath arm, take hold of the opposite thumb. Lift the elbows to shoulder height. Press the elbows forwards and slightly squeeze the forearms into each other.

Prudence: Keep the head and neck in a neutral position. Keep the elbows lifted.

UPPER SHOULDER RELEASE VAR. NO. 1

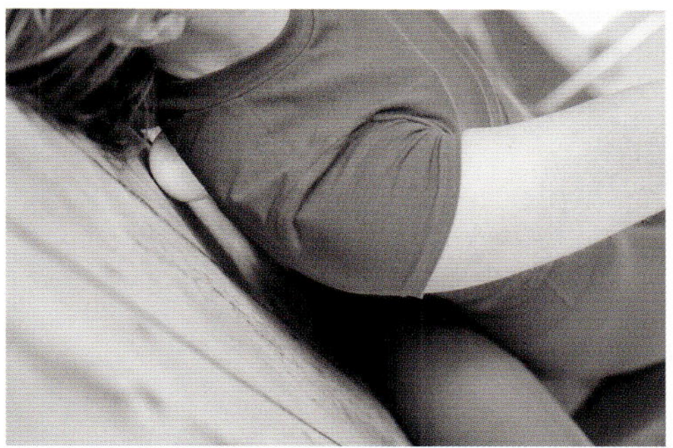

Purpose: To release the upper shoulders.

Prepare: Lie in a constructive rest position. Place a release ball underneath either side of the shoulders. Lift the hips off the ground and place a roller underneath the sacrum.

Perform: Raise your arms towards the ceiling.

Prudence: Place the roller carefully so the lower back feels supported. Make sure the release balls are placed on the muscles either side of the spine, away from the spine itself.

CHILD'S POSE WITH LATERAL FLEXION (STRETCH)

Purpose: To stretch the back and sides of the upper body.

Prepare: Assume an all fours position and sit back onto your heels with your arms outstretched above your head on the floor.

Perform: Walk your hands over to one side. Return to the centre. Alternate the sides as you go through your repetitions.

Prudence: As you reach to the side, press your opposite buttock down to provide an oppositional stretch.

Stool

BETWEEN THE RIB MASSAGE (RELEASE)

Purpose: To release the muscles between the ribs.

Prepare: Sit comfortably on a stool.

Perform: Raise the left arm. Use the opposite hand to trace the ribs to their ending in the front of the body. Apply pressure where it feels sharp.

Prudence: Breathe into any tightness until it lessens.

To summarise, for reaching and rotating, we have used a combination of 1 strengthen, 2 stretch and 3 release, with an emphasis on stretch.

Applying 123 to cardiovascular movement

We have so far focused on applying our 123 Approach to individual muscles and to some day-to-day activities, but how do these relate to cardiovascular exercise? In the following Sections 3, 4 and 5, we will use three variations of our triangle model to apply to three different cardiovascular exercises. You can, in fact, apply any one of these models to any cardiovascular activity. However, we have chosen to link these models to three activities we find most fitting:

Section 3
CYCLING

Section 4
RUNNING

Section 5
SWIMMING

These sections simply allow us the opportunity to present the following models to you. However, as you now know, these models are not fixed. Our aim is to give you a perspective to work with for the most benefit to your body.

Here are the models upfront:

MODEL VARIATION NO. 1

This first model shows an option for strengthening before you exercise and then using stretch and release work for recovery.

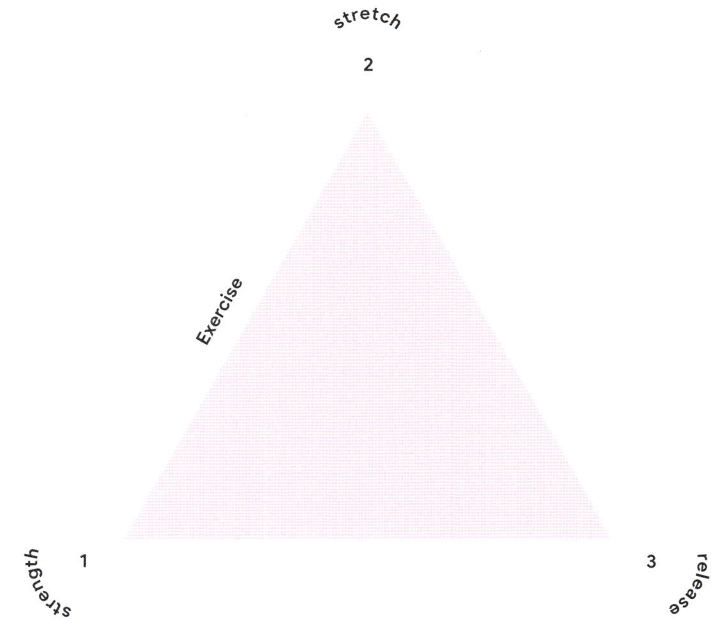

MODEL VARIATION NO. 2

This second model demonstrates using release and strengthening work before you exercise and then using stretch work for recovery. Release work here can be cleverly used to make sure that when you are strengthening a particular area of the body, that you do not strengthen into the wrong area.

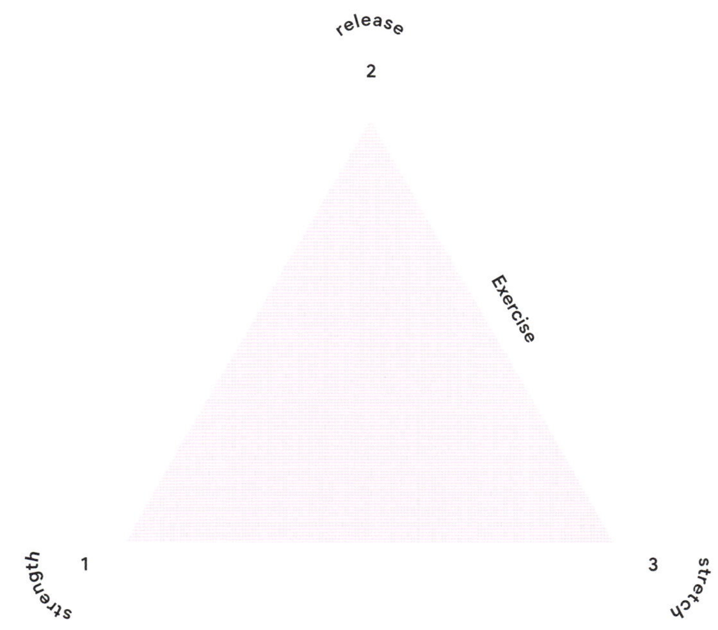

This is a real positive of release work! When areas of the body build tension those areas tend to overwork when you do not need or want them to. This can be to the detriment of activation in other areas and can be a leading cause of injury. In this model, we have added release work as a special emphasis to encourage you to not neglect this area, as it's the least considered of the three choices.

MODEL VARIATION NO. 3

This third model lays down a way to separate out the 123 options. This way you can keep your conditioning work short, but if you cover all three in a day, or spread them across a few days, you will help your body to become strong, flexible, relaxed and responsive to any given situation.

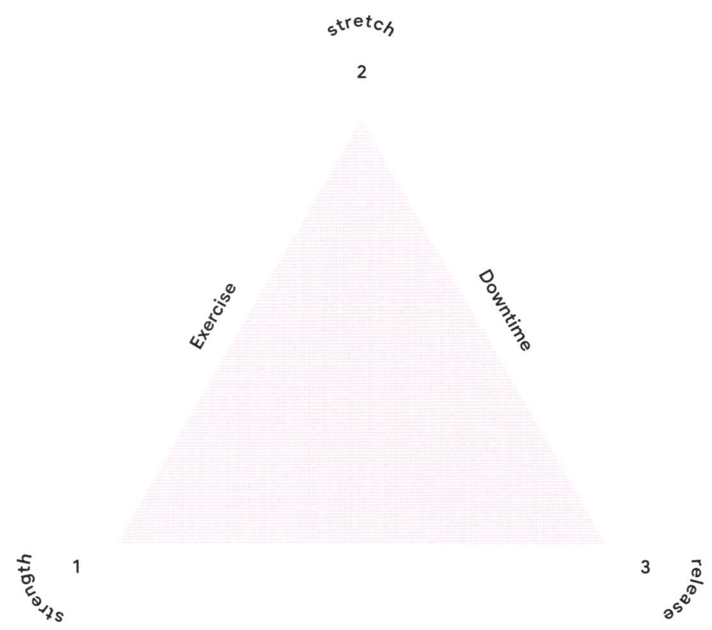

Pick your cardiovascular exercise and match it with one of the models above. As always, our 123 Approach is flexible. Feel free to change the model or apply any variation to a cardiovasacular exercise of your choosing.

Spotlight: Cardiovascular movement and your heart rate

The NHS recommends 150 minutes of moderate activity per week or 75 minutes of vigorous activity. Moderate activity is between 50–70% of your max heart rate, and vigorous activity is 70–85%. To work out your max heart rate, you just subtract your age from 220. Your resting heart rate should be between 60–100 beats per minute. You can check this by taking your pulse just before you get out of bed in the morning. It is useful to understand these figures when contemplating cardiovascular activity. However, some of us just want to get out there and enjoy moving. That is fine too!

Either way, we shall begin to integrate our cardiovascular activities into the centre of our models. It is an option for you to make your chosen cardiovascular activities the leading indicators for what 123 exercises you decide to employ. This will mean your strategies to keep your body working well and feeling good have a clear direction.

CARDIOVASCULAR ACTIVITY	MODERATE	VIGOROUS
MINUTES / WEEK	150	75
% MAX HEART RATE*	50–70%	70–85%

*max heart rate = 220 – [your age]

Section

Applying 123 to cycling

Current exercise trends can seem intimidating to some when contemplating re-engaging with exercise after a break from it. As Pilates and Yoga instructors, we obviously advocate what we teach. However, as dancers and advocates of modern science, we also recognise that Pilates and/or Yoga on their own are not enough. The human body needs its cardiovascular capacity challenged on a regular basis to maintain good heart health and to keep our inner organs functioning well, while Yoga and Pilates are exceptional disciplines for generating and maintaining a good relationship with our body. We want to lay out here the best way to use them together, along with our take on release work, to enjoy optimal exercise and body function.

Assuming you have gotten on top of the areas that need releasing and stretching in the sit to stand section of this book, this is how we might use the triangle for cycling.

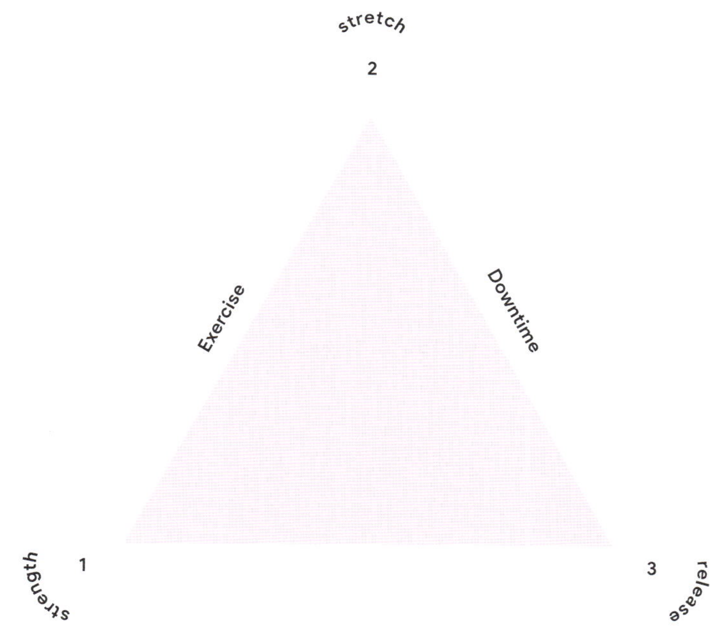

How sit to stand relates to cycling

The muscles involved in sit to stand movements are the buttock muscles, the back of the thigh (hamstrings), the core muscles and the postural muscles of the back. These areas are very similar to the areas that help us when we cycle. The main differences are that when we extend the legs we do so individually when we are cycling, rather than bilaterally as we do when performing a sit to stand.

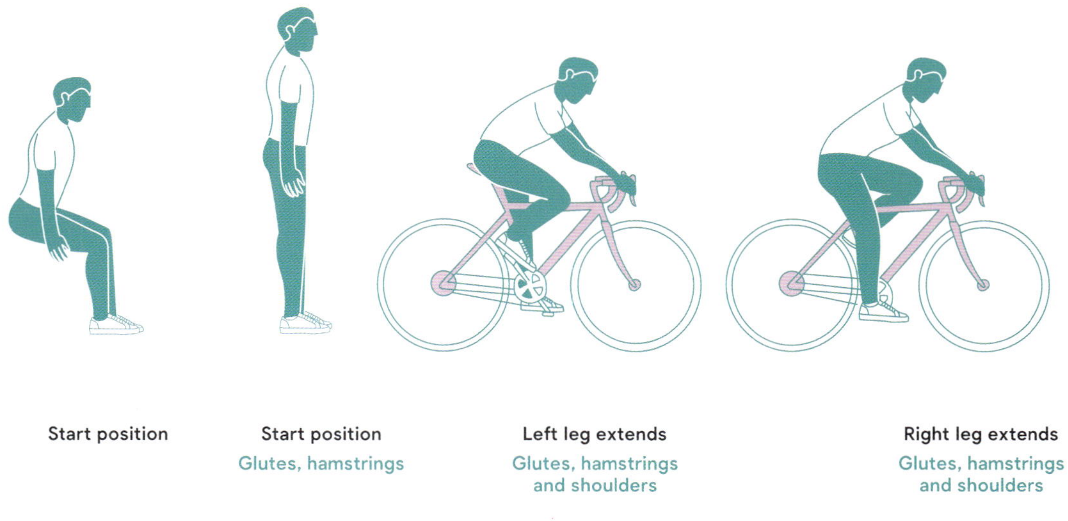

Start position

Start position
Glutes, hamstrings

Left leg extends
Glutes, hamstrings and shoulders

Right leg extends
Glutes, hamstrings and shoulders

Additionally, we also remain in a seated position with our weight on our arms, rather than just using our legs when performing a sit to stand movement. This program develops on from the sit to stand section.

1 Strength

When cycling, the front of our thighs dominate to perform the movement of pedalling. However, if we can activate and utilise the muscles in the back of the hip we will gain more power and stamina, due to the effort load being distributed amongst more areas of the body. Incidentally, this concept applies to sit-to-stand movements, squatting in gym work and activities such as skiing. This makes the information here a useful and versatile concept that is worth taking the time to understand and practise.

Spotlight: Muscles involved in cycling

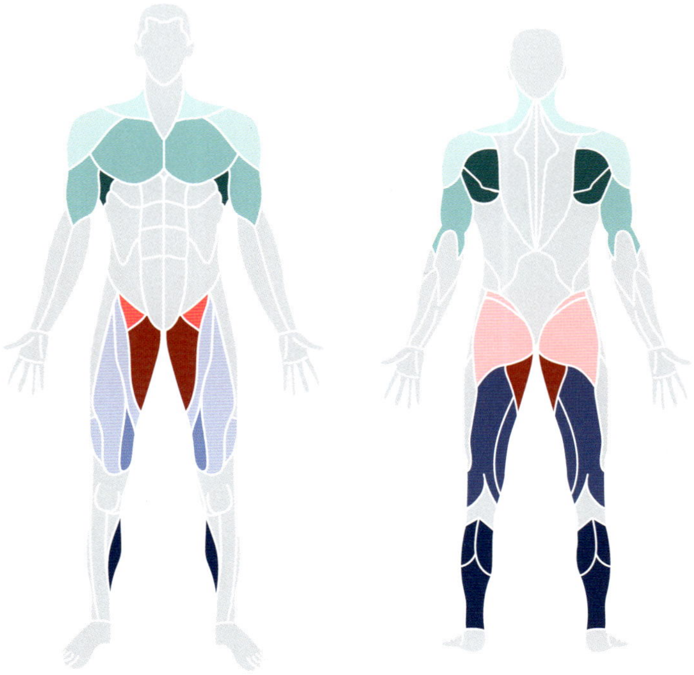

Here we show you an exercise for the area at the lower part of the buttock muscles, which will help maintain the use of the back of the hip. This is important for muscle balance in this area to maintain good hip health. Try this:

Stool

SINGLE LEG SIT TO STAND VAR. NO. 2 (STRENGTH)

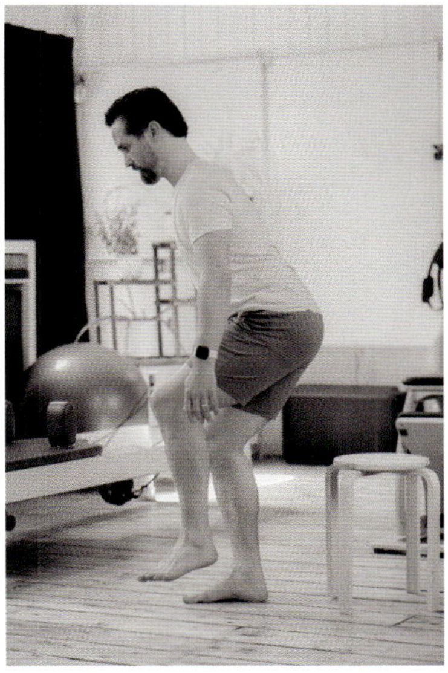

Purpose: To strengthen the buttocks and improve balance.

Prepare: Sit on the front edge of a chair or stool with your feet hip distance apart, spine neutral and shoulders relaxed. Make sure the knee angle of your working leg is no more acute than 90 degrees. Hover your other leg off the floor slightly. Hold onto something if you need to. Folding forward at the hips, once you feel you have enough of a tipping point, press the working foot into the floor to come up to standing.

Perform: Actively squeeze the lower part of the buttock muscle and pulse up and down a few inches. Repeat 30 times before returning to sitting.

Prudence: Keep the spine neutral and maintain the lower buttock muscle activation throughout.

Continuing with the theme of ensuring the back of the legs work to contribute to a cycling movement, here is an exercise for the back of the thighs:

Roller

BRIDGING VAR. NO. 2 (STRENGTH)

Purpose: To work the back of the thighs.

Prepare: Lie in a constructive rest position with the front of your heels on a horizontal roller.

Perform: Squeeze the lower glutes and lift your pelvis until it is in line with your shoulders and knees. Roll the roller towards your hips and away from you again 3 times before lowering back down.

Prudence: Maintain neutral spine. Keep feet and knees in parallel.

Our preferred height for a bike seat is one in which you can almost straighten the knee when the foot is in the downward movement of pedalling. That means we need to work the calves with both a bent knee and a straight knee. Here are two calf exercises to try:

HEEL RAISES VAR. NO. 2 (STRENGTH)

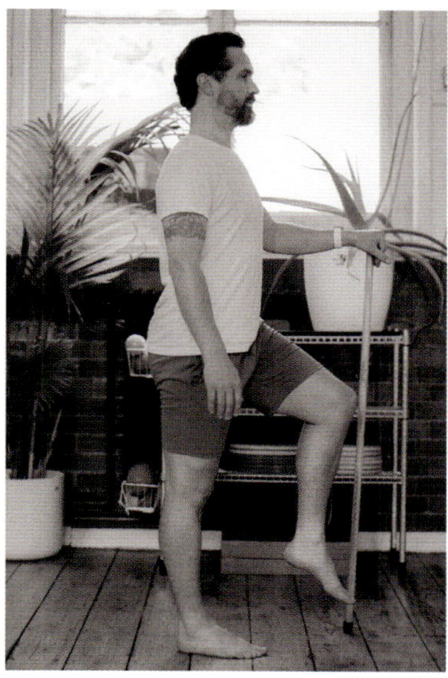
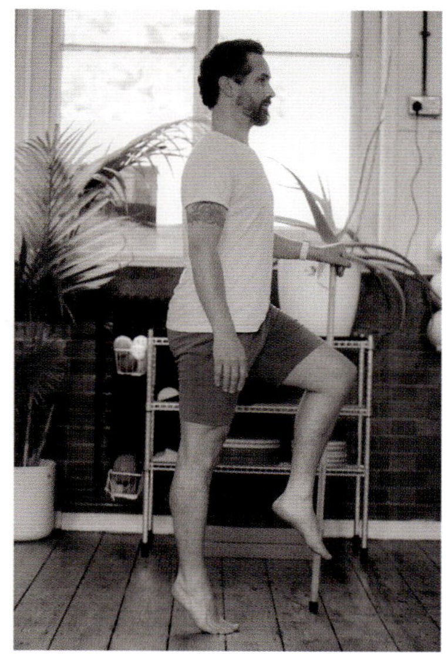

Purpose: To strengthen the lower legs.

Prepare: Stand with your feet hip distance apart and lift one leg up.

Perform: Press down into the balls of the standing foot and slowly raise the heel, then control the heel back down.

Prudence: Use something to hold onto if balance is difficult.

LOWER CALF HEEL RAISES (STRENGTH)

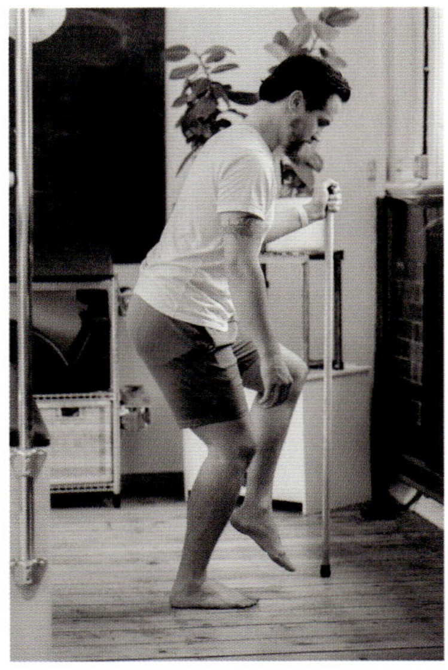

Purpose: To strengthen the deep lower leg muscles.

Prepare: Stand with your feet hip distance apart and knees slightly bent. Lift one leg slightly off the floor. Hold onto a stick for balance if you need to.

Perform: Lift the standing leg heel off the floor as high as you can, resulting in the body lifting in one piece. Lower the heel back down.

Prudence: Keep the weight of the body slightly forward.

Good hip function means that the hip joint slides smoothly inside its socket. One way to ensure this is to utilise the front of the hip muscle, which allows you to both practise this and to warm up that area of the body. Here is a good exercise for this:

KNEE FLOATS VAR. NO. 2 (STRENGTH)

Purpose: To strengthen the hip flexors.

Prepare: Lie on your back with your knees bent, legs parallel.

Perform: Raise one leg slowly, bringing the knee above the hip, then lift the other leg to join it before lowering the legs back down, one at a time.

Prudence: Keep the pelvis and spine neutral and the upper body relaxed. Vary the side you start on.

Functional shoulder stability helps keep our upper torso in a good position whilst cycling. Here is a common exercise that helps with this:

PLANKING (STRENGTH)

Purpose: Full body strengthening with a strong focus on the arms and core.

Prepare: On all fours place your shoulders over your wrists and your hips above the knees.

Perform: Step your legs back one at a time into a plank position. Lengthen through the arms and slightly draw the tummy in. Be sure to keep the pelvis level and spine neutral.

Prudence: Keep a light engagement of the abdominal muscles to maintain a neutral lower back.

Planking (Strength)

As with the sit to stand movement, it's important to keep the front of the thigh muscles balanced, rather than letting the outside thigh muscles dominate. Here is an exercise for the inner front of thigh muscle:

Inflatable ball + cushion

INNER FRONT OF THIGH VAR. NO. 2 (STRENGTH)

Purpose: To strengthen the innermost front thigh muscle.

Prepare: Lie on your back with a roller or inflatable ball underneath the back of the thighs. You may want to use cushions to support your head.

Perform: Straighten one leg. Flex the foot, turn the leg out slightly from the hip, then take the leg slightly across the body over the opposite hip. Bring the leg back, return the leg to neutral position, relax the foot and then lower the foot back down.

Prudence: Make sure when you straighten the leg that you draw up the inner quad muscle and feel it tense. You can check this by feeling the muscle with your hand.

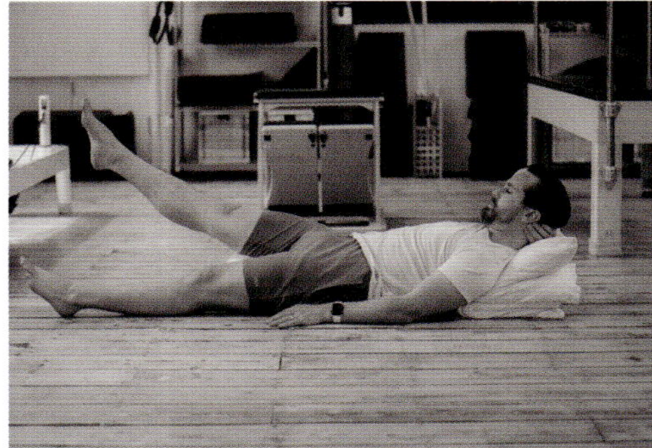

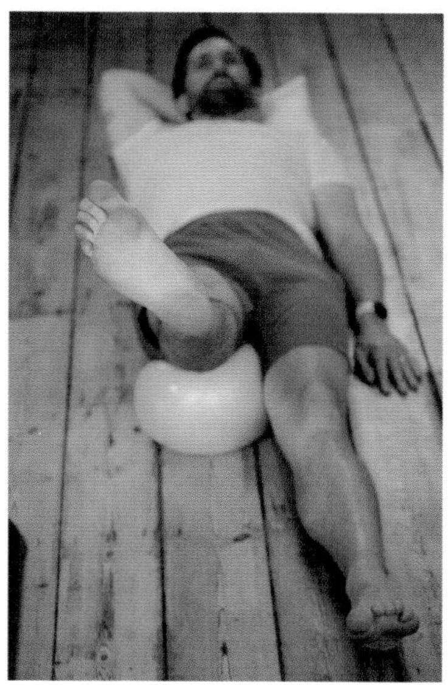

Now your body is prepared, you can go for a cycle.

Go for a cycle

2 Stretch

Cycling is a great cardiovascular activity. You get to use the big muscles in your legs, which require more oxygenated blood than the smaller muscles in your body. This means that it is easy to build up a sweat and work on your lung capacity quickly. Cycling is increasingly becoming a popular means of getting from A to B. With more public conscientiousness around environmental issues it makes us feel, and rightly so, that we are doing our bit for the planet. But getting yourself around can build up tension. So, to maintain this wonderful physical activity, you will need to know how to, and where to, stretch out.

In the previous pages we have covered the exercises that we would recommend when preparing for cycling as they will help you to:

- Warm up the key areas to not 'pull a muscle'.
- Help you to activate the correct muscles when performing the movement of cycling.
- Maintain muscle balance by working the areas of the body in a balanced way.
- Build the right tension, in the right areas, to get you ready to cycle.

But how can we ease off the tension built up from cycling through stretch and release work? In the following sequence of exercises, we will address the tension that can build up in the lower back.

Spotlight: Muscles to stretch after cycling

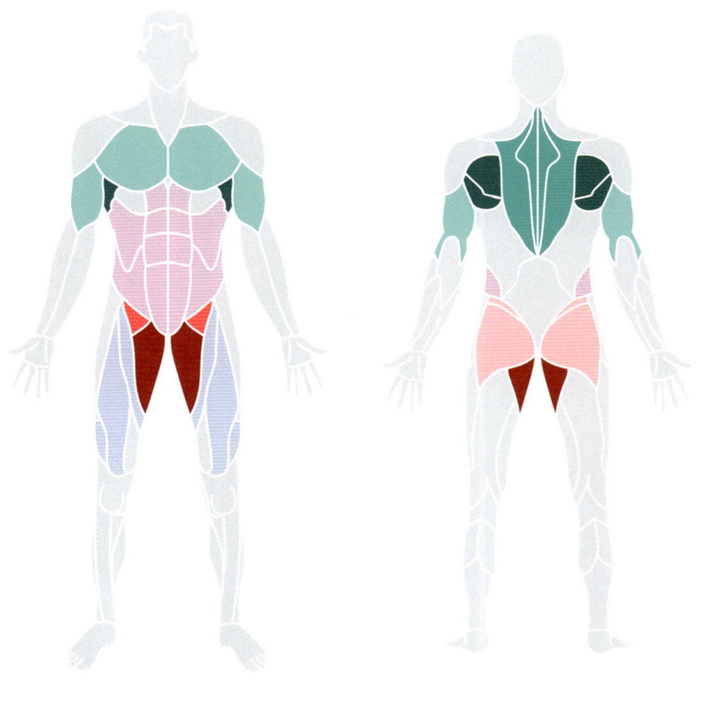

Because we have been using the big muscles of the thighs, we tend to build up tension in the lower back. This is a good exercise to begin this stretch sequence:

CAT STRETCH VAR. NO. 2

Purpose: To stretch the back and mobilise the upper spine.

Prepare: Assume an all fours position but bring your hands closer to your knees this time.

Perform: Draw your navel in and round your back. Return to a neutral spine. Repeat 10 times.

Prudence: Relax the back of your neck.

Cat stretch var. no. 2

Stabilising your shoulders correctly requires gently drawing your shoulder blades down your back. However, this leads to the sides of the body getting tight. This next exercise helps stretch this area out.

Stool

TEAPOT (STRETCH)

Purpose: To stretch the side of your body and the back of your upper arms.

Prepare: Sit on a chair or stool and place the palm of one hand between your shoulder blades with your elbow pointing towards the ceiling. Place your other hand on top of that elbow.

Perform: Lift in your waist and lean away from the elbow that is pointing towards the ceiling, bringing your body into a side bend. Alternate sides as you go through your repetitions.

Prudence: Keep your pelvis level and facing forward, imagining you are standing in between 2 panes of glass.

HAPPY CYCLIST POSE (STRETCH)

Purpose: To stretch the inner, and back of, thighs.

Prepare: Lie in a constructive rest position.

Perform: Bring your knees into your chest, pointing the soles of your feet to the ceiling. Hands on ankles and open knees. Press the sacrum down and maintain neutral spine.

Prudence: Let your body dictate how far into the stretch you push.

The big buttock muscles will be a huge factor in lower back tension. Here is how we can deal with them through stretching:

PIGEON VAR. NO. 2 (STRETCH)

Purpose: To stretch the back and side of the hip.

Prepare: Assume an all fours position.

Perform: Place the left knee on the floor on the outside of the left hand and place the left foot on the floor close to the right hip, resulting in the outside of the left lower leg having contact with the floor. Slide the right leg back along the floor away from the hands and the lower right hip towards the floor. Rest the body over your left leg, reaching the hands forward along the floor. Rest in this position.

Prudence: If you experience discomfort in the knee or lower back, choose another glute stretch that we have recommended. Try to keep the pelvis level with the floor.

After the continuous folding forward in the waist positioning of cycling, coupled with the tightening of the chest from supporting some of your body weight with the arms, this opening the front of the body exercise will help ease things off:

2 blocks

KNEELING FRONT BODY STRETCH

Purpose: To stretch the front of the hips, waist and chest.

Prepare: Kneel upright with your hands on the back of the pelvis. Have a block in each hand (or you could use a couple of same-size books).

Perform: Push the pelvis forward and lift the chest up and the back into an arched position. Place the blocks on the floor either side of each foot in an upright position, shoulder width apart. Let the head release back.

Prudence: Keep the buttock and core muscles engaged to about 50% effort.

Kneeling front body stretch

No matter how much we engage the backs of the thighs, the front of thigh muscles will always take on more of the load when cycling. This is an easy time-tested stretch for that area of the body:

FRONT OF THIGH STRETCH VAR. NO. 1

Purpose: To stretch the front of the thighs.

Prepare: Stand upright with feet hip distance apart.

Perform: Bend one knee to take the foot back and up towards the same-side buttock. Take hold of the foot with the same-side hand.

Prudence: Draw the tummy in and up to support the lower back and stay in a neutral position.

The front of the hip could do with some extra attention after the folded forward cycling position. This can really allow you to stretch into that area:

LOW LUNGE VAR. NO. 2 (STRETCH)

Purpose: To stretch the front of the hip and thigh.

Prepare: Take a deep lunge back with one leg.

Perform: Tuck the pelvis and lift the same arm as the leg that's back towards the ceiling. Lift out of the waist and reach up and over towards the space above the bent leg. Breathe deeply for 10 breaths. Return to upright and then standing.

Prudence: Stack the front knee over the front ankle.

3 Release

The stretches covered in the previous sequence can help to re-lengthen your muscles after the muscles contraction that is demanded when cycling. They can also help to decrease the inevitable lactic acid build up, or DOMS (delayed onset muscle stiffness). Another way of minimising DOMS is release work. Let us look at a programme for that designed to help with cycling.

After stretching at the end of a cycle, whilst your body is still warm, it wouldn't be a bad idea to save your release work until later in the day or evening. You don't need a warm-up to perform these exercises, and you can also do them alongside your stretching.

Spotlight: Muscles to release after cycling

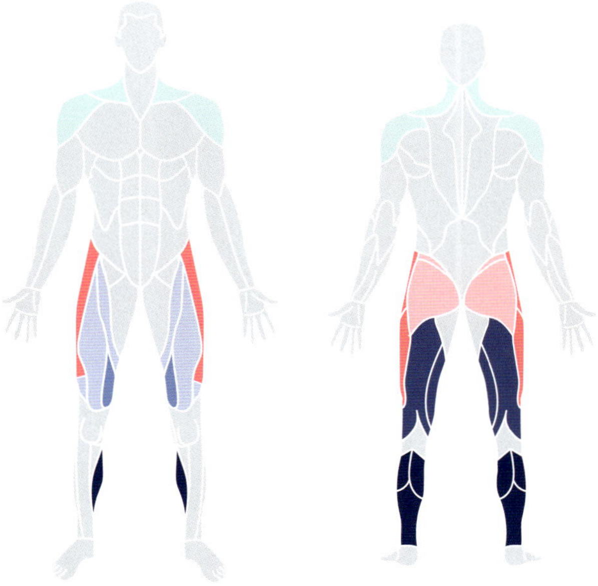

The outside of the thighs can often tighten up when cycling, for reasons we have mentioned earlier. Particularly, when the lateral front of thigh muscles tend to dominate. This exercise can contribute to warding off that scenario:

Roller

ROLL OUTSIDE OF THIGH VAR. NO. 1 (RELEASE)

Purpose: To release the outside of the thigh.

Prepare: Lie on your side with a roller under your bottom thigh, propping yourself up with the underneath elbow.

Perform: Keeping the foot of the top leg on the floor, use that leg and your elbow to roll up and down the thigh.

Prudence: Keep the head and neck aligned with your spine. Stay in between the hip joint and knee joint.

An obvious area to release is the buttock muscles. We have discussed how these muscles extend the hip, or propel us forward, in cycling, so here is a release for them:

Release ball

BUTTOCK MUSCLES RELEASE VAR. NO. 4

Purpose: To release the buttock muscles.

Prepare: Sit on the floor with your knees bent and place a release ball on the upper part of the buttock muscles, resting back on the hands as indicated.

Perform: Once a tight spot is found, rest there for 10 deep breaths. Try to find different trigger point positions.

Prudence: Remain on the muscle, not bone or joints.

Provided that you are using enough of your calves when cycling (see the activation exercises on pages 115–116), they may need releasing. If they feel sensitive, it is a strong sign that there is a build up of tension. Try this:

Release ball + block

LOWER LEG RELEASE VAR. NO. 2

Purpose: To release the deep lower leg muscles.

Prepare: Place a release ball on top of a block (or you could simply stack a pile of 3 or 4 books).

Perform: Sit on the floor and place 1 lower leg on the ball and the other leg on top to add more weight. Rest there briefly, and then move the ball to a different spot on the lower leg.

Prudence: Keep the ball below the main bulk of the calf and above the Achilles.

The lower back muscles will benefit from release work in the evening as they can often tighten up overnight after a cycle. This is a great exercise to tackle the lower back muscles:

Release ball

SINGLE SIDE BACK RELEASE

Purpose: To release the muscles that extend the back.

Prepare: Lie in a constructive rest position with your hands behind your head.

Perform: Place a single ball on one side of the spine just below the shoulder. Once a tight spot is found, take 10 deep breaths. Move 1cm down the back and repeat. Continue down the spine until you reach the pelvis.

Prudence: Stay off any bones, especially your spine.

The outside of the hip muscle is responsible for tightening up the area on the outside of the thigh. This release works well combined with the outside of thigh release (see page 167).

Release ball

OUTSIDE OF HIP RELEASE VAR. NO. 2

Purpose: To release the outside of the hip.

Prepare: Lie on your side with the top knee bent and bottom knee straight. Rest your head on your bottom arm.

Perform: Place a release ball under your hip in between the front of the hip bone and the top of your outside thigh bones. Take 10 deep breaths before exploring a slightly different spot that is also tight.

Prudence: Stay on the muscle and avoid the bone.

One area that has a big impact on pelvis position, and therefore lower back tension, is the back of the thigh. Here is a good release for this area:

Stool + block + release ball

BACK OF THIGH RELEASE VAR. NO. 2

Purpose: To release the lateral back of the thigh muscle.

Prepare: Sit on a chair or stool where the lower legs can dangle.

Perform: Place a release ball in the belly of the lateral back of thigh muscle. Rest your foot on top of a block (or you could use a pile of books). Then, place your hands on your thighs and apply pressure. Explore trigger points along the length of the muscle.

Prudence: This muscle can be slippery, so stay on the tubular shape of the muscle and stay away from bone and joints.

Please see page 53 for how to locate the lateral Hamstring.

Finally, these next two releases for the front of the thighs will reset the tension in this area. If these areas get overtight, they can both have an impact on the knee joints functionality and can result in pain.

Roller

ROLL FRONT OF THIGH (RELEASE)

Purpose: To release the front of the thigh.

Prepare: Lie on your front, propping yourself up with your elbows, with one leg out straight and one leg bent. Place a roller underneath the straight leg.

Perform: Roll back and forth on the front thigh of the extended leg.

Prudence: Encourage the shoulder blades to draw down your back.

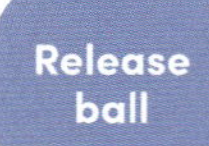

INSIDE FRONT OF THIGH RELEASE

Purpose: To release the inside front of the thigh muscle.

Prepare: Lie on your front with one leg straight and one knee bent out to the side.

Perform: Place a release ball under the inside front of the thigh muscle near your knee.

Prudence: Stay on the muscle and avoid bones or joints.

In summary, we believe these exercises will keep your body 'in good nick' if cycling is your thing. Remember the simple concept of the 123 Approach and make sure you are getting a good balance of exercises in the areas of 1 strength, 2 stretch and 3 release work.

Section

Applying 123 to running

Assuming you have gotten on top of the areas that need releasing and stretching in the walking section of this book, this is how we might use the triangle for running. Running is an incredible way to partake in cardiovascular activity. It burns 50% more calories than walking. So if you are strapped for time to exercise, this is a worthwhile endeavour. You must make sure you have good knee, ankle and hip joints as it is a relatively high-impact activity. One of the benefits of this high impact is that it improves bone density, which diminishes as we age. One of the biggest predictors of physical decline is falls in the elderly. When this happens, they can often break bones due to the low bone density. Along with improving your bone density, running also helps with balance, so this is a no-brainer choice of activity, even in small measures, if your joints are on board with it.

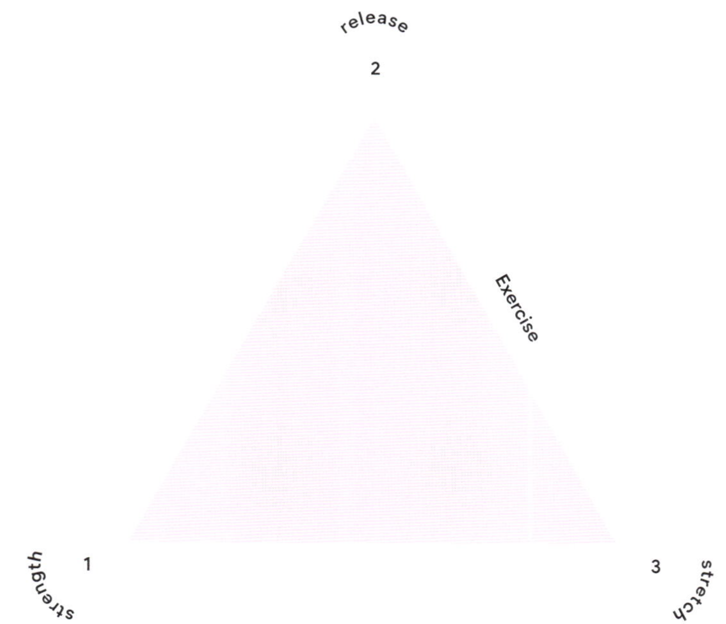

How walking relates to running

As we saw in the section on walking, the hip needs to extend behind the body to propel us forward. That means stretching the front of the hip and working the muscles in the back of the thigh simultaneously. We also rotate our torso to counterbalance our bodies, so we don't fall over. We achieve this by working the muscles in the sides of the waist. We also push off the feet, using the muscles in the back of the lower legs.

When we run, we use the same areas of the body to achieve movement as when we walk. The only difference is that we put more effort in. Enough effort to achieve a moment between each step when the entire body is suspended off the ground. As such, we will use similar exercises to when we were looking at walking, but we will increase the exercises' intensity as a preparation for running.

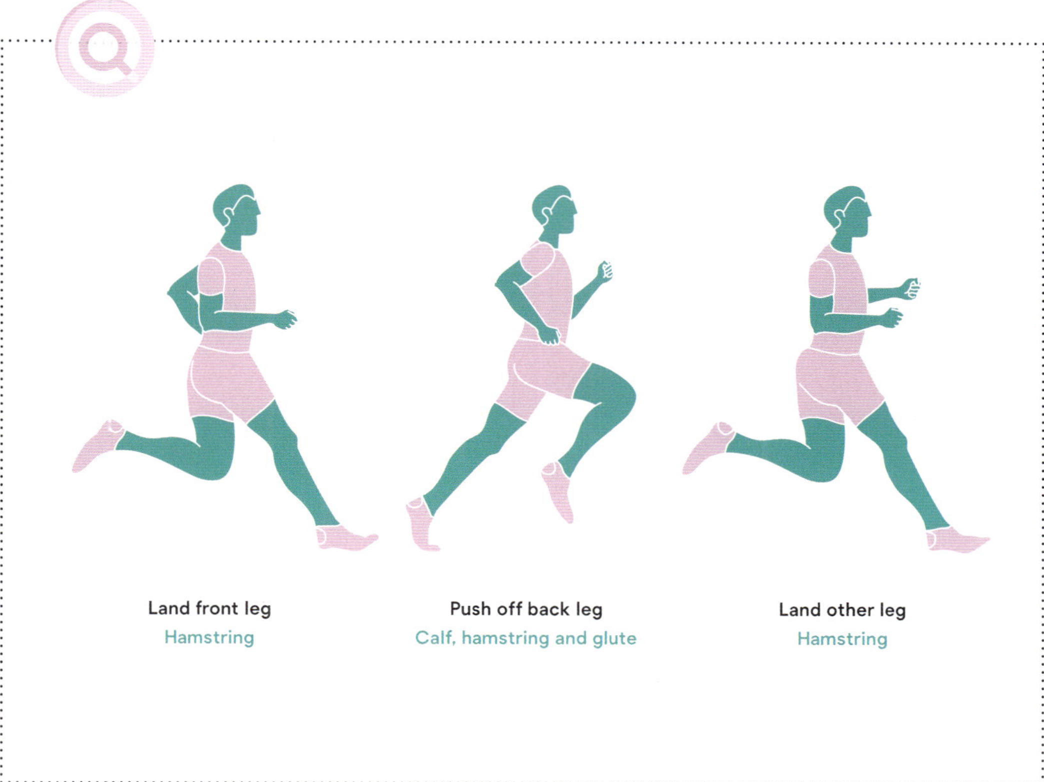

1 Strength

Even if your knees, ankles and hips are in good condition, you still need to consider a level of muscle activation before you begin running. This will enable these joints to remain in good condition. When we activate muscles we give the joints support, so the joints do not have to take all the strain. The muscles work from the outset to hold the bones of the joints away from one another. Let's have a look at some exercises to get us going.

Spotlight: Muscles involved in running

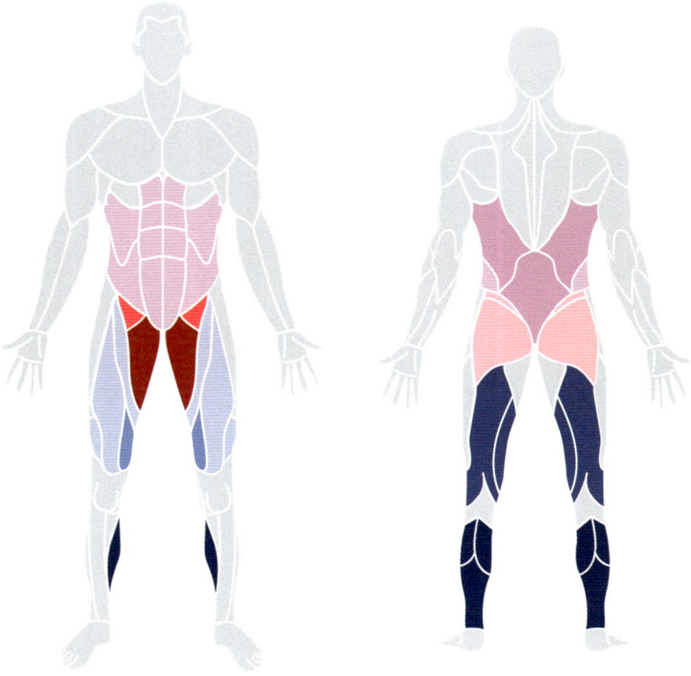

This single leg sit to stand exercise can be developed for use without a stool. That means it will challenge your balance more whilst making your muscles work harder.

Stool

SINGLE LEG SIT TO STAND VAR. NO. 3 (STRENGTH)

Purpose: To improve hip mobility, strengthen the buttocks and improve balance.

Prepare: Sit on the front edge of a chair or stool with your feet hip distance apart, spine neutral and the shoulders relaxed. Keep the angle of the working leg no more acute than 90 degrees. Hover your other leg off the floor slightly. Hold on to something if you need to.

Perform: Actively squeeze the lower part of your buttock muscles. Folding forward at the hips, once you feel you have enough of a tipping point, press the working foot into the floor to come up to standing. Open your lifted leg out to the side, return the leg to parallel, and then sit back down.

Prudence: Keep your spine neutral and maintain lower glute activation throughout.

This variation on the bridging exercise will work the back of the thigh more intensely:

BRIDGING VAR. NO. 3 (STRENGTH)

Purpose: To strengthen the back of the thighs.

Prepare: Lie in a constructive rest position with your feet on the floor.

Perform: Squeeze the lower buttock muscles. Lift your pelvis until it is in line with your shoulders and knees. Lift one knee into tabletop. Open the knee of the leg that is on the floor out to the side and back in again. Repeat this in-and-out motion up to 8 times before placing the other foot back on the floor and lowering the hips back down.

Prudence: Maintain a neutral spine. Keep the feet and knees in parallel.

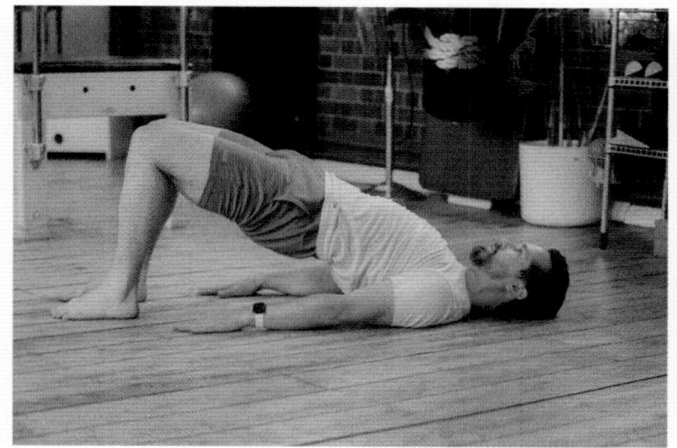

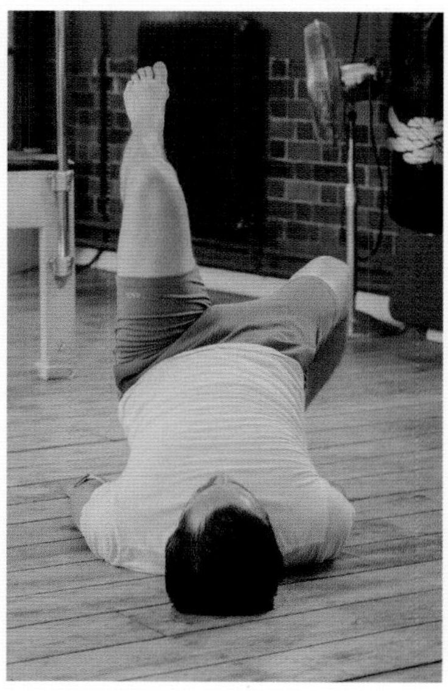
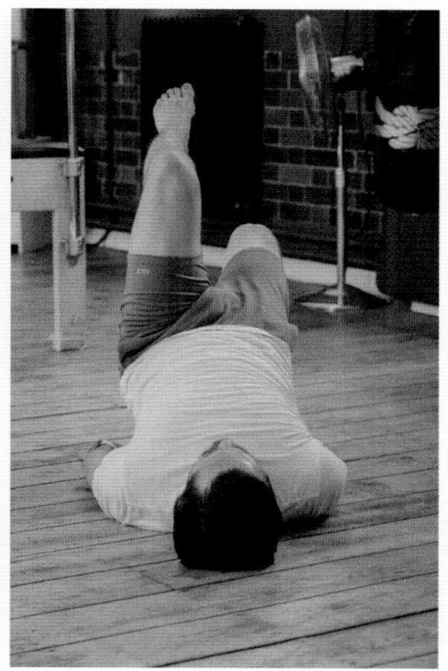

Bridging var. no. 3 (Strength)

This variation of the knee float exercise (see page 65) is to target the deep core muscles. This exercise utilises the weight of the legs to challenge and strengthen this area more:

KNEE FLOATS VAR. NO. 3 (STRENGTH)

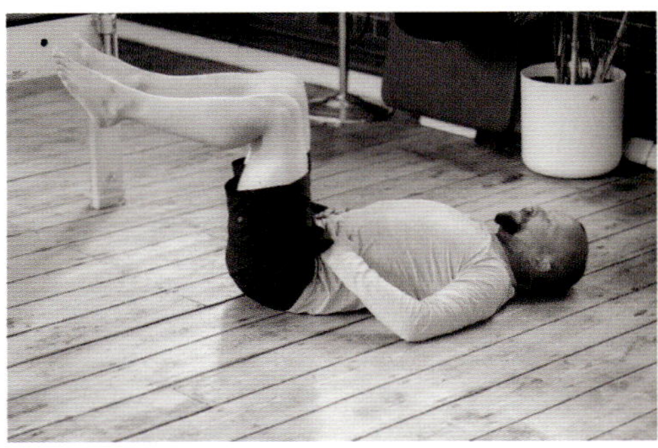

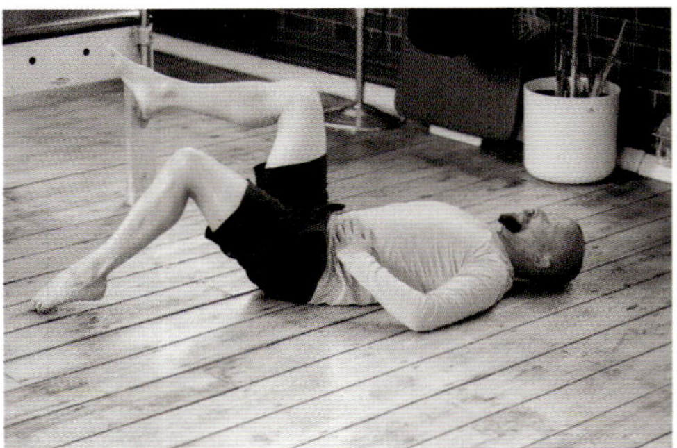

Purpose: To strengthen and connect to deep core muscles.

Prepare: Lie down with your knees above your hips and shins horizontal. Place your hands below your navel.

Perform: Lower one leg to lightly touch the floor with your toes, then slowly bring the knee back above the hip. Alternate the sides as you go through your repetitions.

Prudence: Maintain a neutral spine and keep the same amount of bend in the knees.

By performing these next two exercises on a single leg, this mimics the intensity needed for the push-off part using the back leg when running.

Mat + sticks

HEEL RAISES VAR. NO. 3 (STRENGTH)

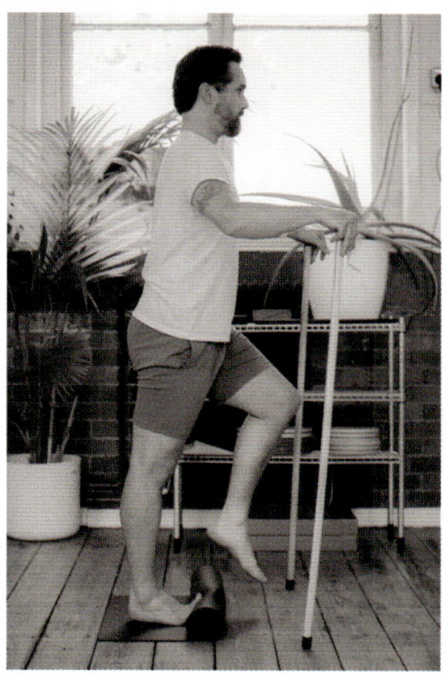

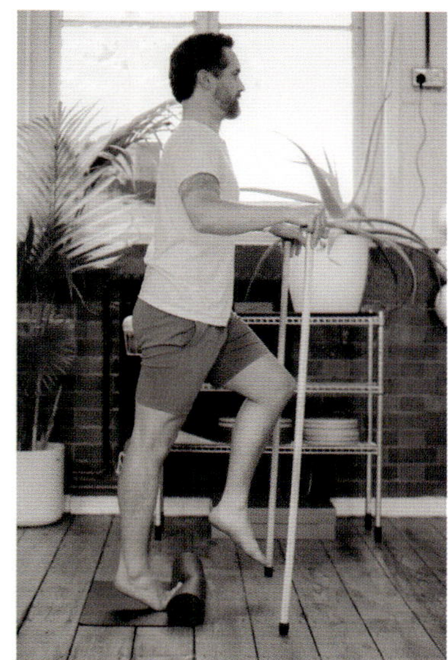

Purpose: To strengthen the lower legs and underside of the feet.

Prepare: Stand with your feet hip distance apart. Raise the toes of one foot using a rolled-up exercise mat, towel or cushion and lift your other leg slightly. Hold on to something for support.

Perform: Press down into the ball of the standing foot and slowly raise the heel, then control the heel back down.

Prudence: Keep the body aligned in neutral.

BENT LEG HEEL RAISES VAR. NO. 2 (STRENGTH)

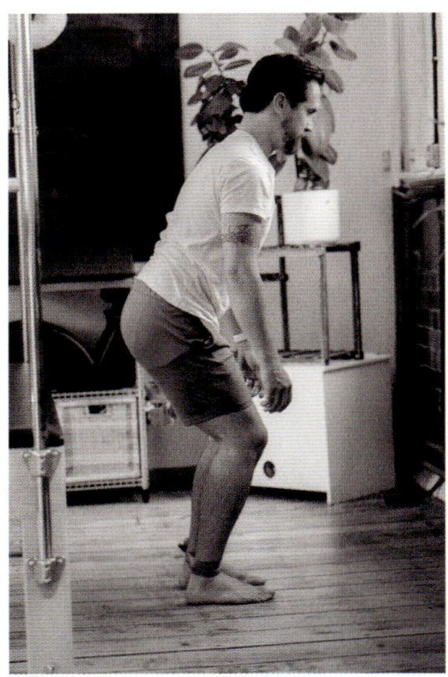

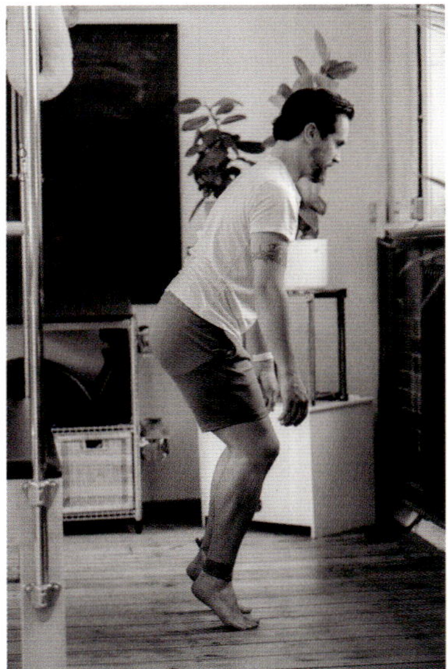

Purpose: To strengthen the deep lower leg muscles.

Prepare: Securely strap a TheraBand around the ankles. Stand with your feet hip distance apart and knees slightly bent, making sure there is some level of resistance in the TheraBand.

Perform: Lift the heels off the floor as high as you can, resulting in the body lifting in one piece. Lower the heels back down.

Prudence: Keep the weight of your body slightly forward.

By adding in a reach with the arms, you should feel the obliques working in a way that feels tougher for the waist. Here's a great exercise for strengthening the oblique muscles:

OBLIQUE CURLS VAR. NO. 2 (STRENGTH)

Purpose: To strengthen the obliques.

Prepare: Assume a constructive rest position and place your hands behind your head.

Perform: Pull the lower tummy in as you lift your head and shoulders and rotate your upper body in one direction. Reach the arms out, joining your hands together on the outside of the leg you have rotated towards. Stay lifted and turn to reach the arms forwards between the legs. Rotate to the other side and reach your arms in that direction. Return the hands behind the head and lower down. Alternate the sides as you go through your repetitions.

Prudence: Bring both shoulder blades off the floor when you lift. Maintain a relaxed neck.

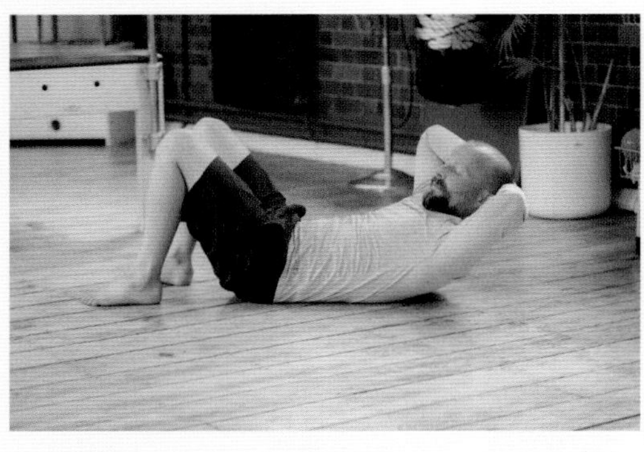
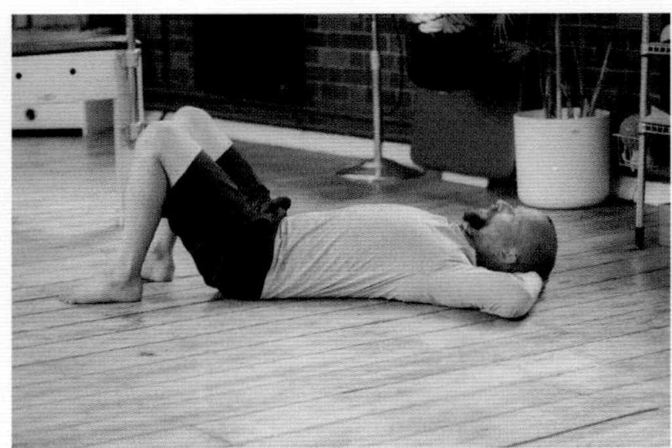

Oblique curls var. no. 2 (Strength)

It is important to feel the connection of the arms into the back for running, just like when walking. This exercise will help you practise the sensation of that connection.

TheraBand

IN FRONT PULLS VAR. NO. 1 (STRENGTH)

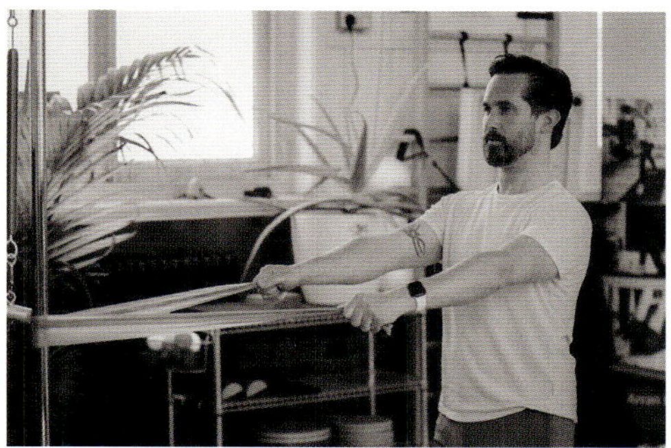

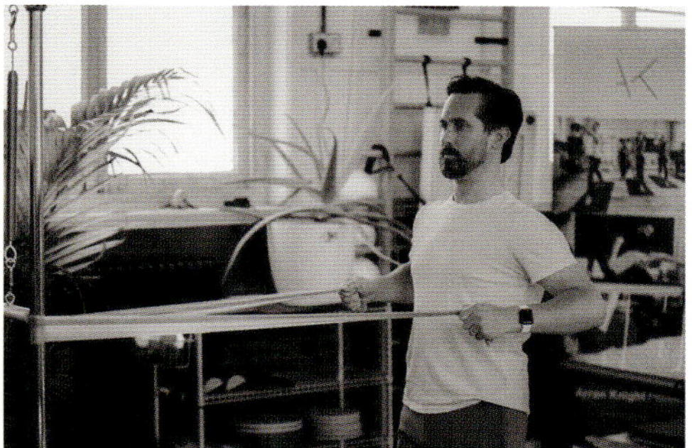

Purpose: To strengthen the areas below the shoulder blades and improve shoulder blade connection to the back.

Prepare: Wrap a TheraBand around an immoveable surface. Stand with your feet hip distance apart, arms outstretched, taking hold of the ends of the TheraBand. Make sure that you have positioned yourself far enough away from the fixed point to have a little bit of tension in the band. Return the arms to the starting position.

Perform: Draw the tummy in gently. Pull your hands in towards you, feeling the back work.

Prudence: Keep the spine neutral.

An addition of a lift in the heel whilst trying to drag the floor towards you with your toes will prepare the feet more thoroughly for a push off the ground, and the articulation needed for landing through the heel and the foot. Try this:

Stool

DOMING FEET (STRENGTH)

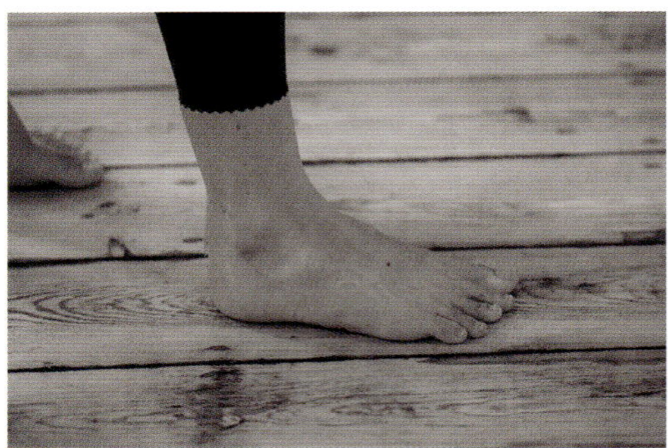

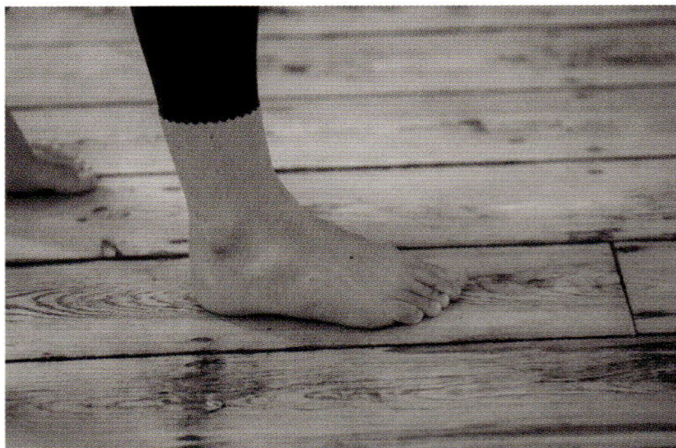

Purpose: To work the underside of your feet.

Prepare: Sit on a stool with knees bent at 90 degrees and feet flat on the floor.

Perform: Press your toes into the floor whilst lifting the balls of the toes away from the floor. Try to narrow the knuckles of the foot whilst trying to drag the floor towards the heels with the toes.

Prudence: Work one foot at a time until confident and keep the front of the ankle relaxed.

We are adding in a mobilising exercise at this stage to open the front of the hip:

LEG SWINGS (STRENGTH)

Purpose: To mobilise the hips and lengthen the hip flexors.

Prepare: Stand your left foot on the floor. Rest your left hand on a wall or stable object and let the left leg hang.

Perform:

a) Swing the left leg back and forth from the hip joint.
b) Imagine your leg begins in your lower back and swing from there.
c) Now, imagine your leg begins all the way up in the thoracic region of the back and swing from there.

Repeat a, b and c 10 times each.

Prudence: Maintain abdominal support to help stabilise the lower back.

2 Release

Tensions can develop in the hip flexor, the outside front of the hip and the outside of the thigh when running. If these areas get tight, it can adversely affect knee-tracking, hip function and pelvis position (and thus increase lower back tension). Therefore, we suggest releasing these areas before you go for a run.

Spotlight: Muscles to release after running

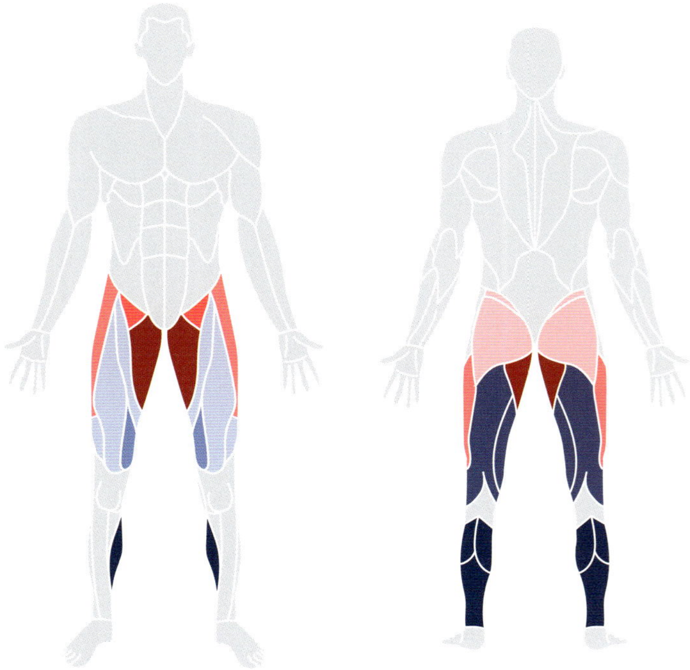

ROLL OUTSIDE OF THIGH VAR. NO. 2 (RELEASE)

Purpose: To release the outer thigh.

Prepare: Lie on your side with a foam roller underneath the outer thigh. Support yourself with the forearm of the lower arm and top hand.

Perform: Roll slowly up and down the outer thigh.

Prudence: Stick to the middle third of the leg, avoiding the knee and hip joints.

Spotlight: Knee health

Believe it or not, the outside of the thigh muscle is a knee stabiliser. It is like an insurance policy that kicks in when your buttock and back of thigh muscles are not strong. If this outside of hip muscle grips consistently, it pulls on the outside of the thigh fascia (which we rolled out on page 161), and in turn can affect knee-tracking. If you keep your buttock muscles and back of thigh muscles strong, this mechanism does not tend to kick in. This, coupled with releasing the outside top of the hip muscle and rolling the outside thigh, is a good strategy to promote long-term knee health.

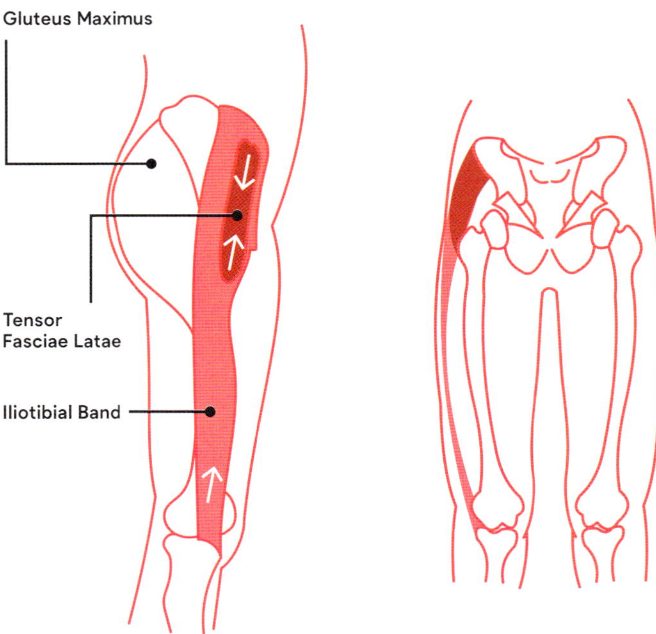

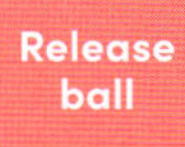

OUTSIDE OF HIP RELEASE VAR. NO. 3

Purpose: To release the outside of the hip.

Prepare: Lie on your side with a release ball in your hand and knees slightly bent. Use the bottom arm to rest your head on.

Perform: Place the ball under the hip in between the front of the hip bones and the top of your outside thigh bones. Experiment with straightening and bending the knee of the bottom leg to track and ease out tension.

Prudence: Stay on muscle and avoid bone.

DEEP HIP FLEXOR RELEASE VAR. NO. 2

Purpose: To release the hip flexors.

Prepare: Lie in a constructive rest position and place your hands on the waist either side of the navel. From var. no. 1 on page 74, you should know where to press into.

Perform: Slowly press one hand into the waist on the same side, then pull out away from the navel.

Prudence: Aim to do this with an empty stomach.

Please see page 73 for how to locate the Psoas muscle

Now you have the body prepared for a run, you can enjoy it with confidence!

Go for a run

3 Stretch

Upon returning from your run, you will have developed tension that needs addressing. The first port of call again is a stretch whilst the body is warm. The lower leg will have taken a lot of repetitive loading and is a good place to start. These next two stretches will loosen the tension developed in this area. Both stretches also offer you the opportunity to open your breathing into your back whilst allowing your breath to settle. Additionally, it is also economical to let gravity do its work in these stretches.

Spotlight: Muscles to stretch after running

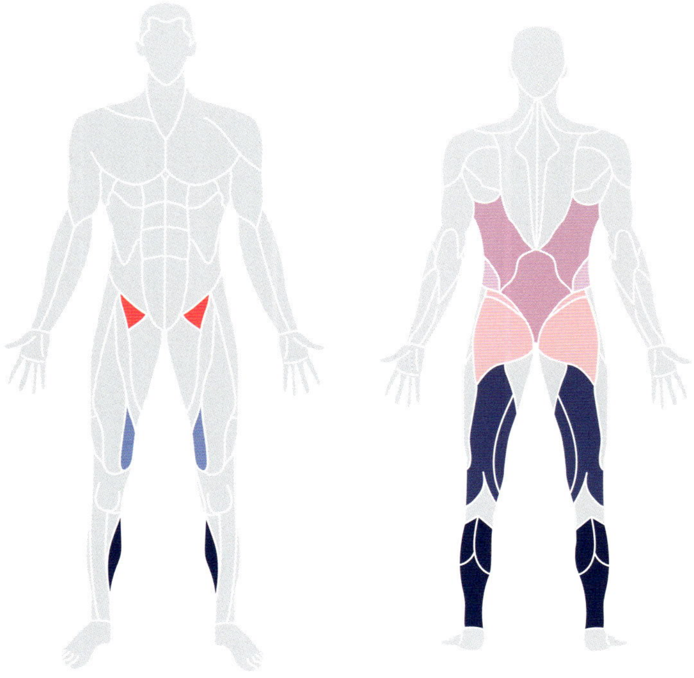

LOWER CALF STRETCH

Purpose: To stretch the lower back of the lower leg.

Prepare: Kneel in a small lunge with one foot in front of the other.

Perform: Adjust the bend in the knees to keep most of the weight on the front foot and find the stretch.

Prudence: Keep the shoulder blades down the back.

TOP OF LOWER LEG STRETCH

Purpose: To stretch the top of the lower leg.

Prepare: From an all fours position, tuck the toes under, straighten the legs and lift your hips into the air.

Perform: Bend one knee slightly, allowing that heel to lift off the floor. Keeping the other knee straight, feel a stretch around the top of the lower leg. Walk through the feet in this fashion, alternating sides as you go through your repetitions.

Prudence: Let the weight of your head go to help relax the neck.

This next stretch is a bit more dynamic in opening the front of the hip and offers the opportunity to re-test your balance after your run. You can identify whether the muscle usage has led to greater stability or not.

DANCER'S POSE (STRETCH)

Purpose: To stretch the front of the hips and thighs.

Prepare: Lift the right foot, bringing the heel to the buttock and taking hold of the outside of the foot with the right hand. Reach the left arm up to the ceiling.

Perform: Press the right foot into the right hand. Take the right leg back as you allow the body to pivot forwards from the left hip. Simultaneously lift the right foot up towards the ceiling as you lift your chest. To return, allow the chest and right thigh to drop towards the floor. Let go of the foot and proceed to then return to upright, standing on both legs.

Prudence: Keep drawing in the stomach muscles to support the lower spine.

With all that hip extension, it's important to stretch out the back of the thighs and hips. Here's a great exercise to do that:

Stretch strap + cushion

BACK OF THIGH STRETCH VAR. NO. 2

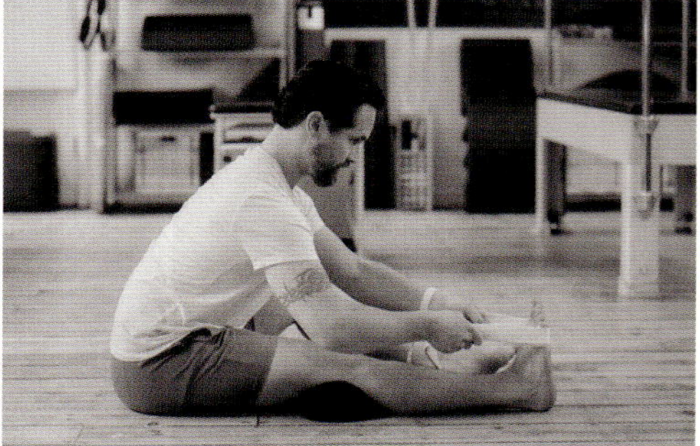

Purpose: To stretch the back of the leg.

Prepare: Sit upright with one leg stretched out and the other leg slightly bent and dropped out to the side. Place a cushion under the knee of the leg that is out straight. Wrap a strap around the foot of the extended leg and hold on to either end with your hands. Make sure there is some tension in the strap.

Perform: Pull on the strap, bending the elbows and folding forwards towards the foot. Hold for up to 10 breaths. Release the stretch and repeat 3 times before changing sides.

Prudence: Take your time to move into the stretch, keeping the spine neutral.

This next hip stretch also addresses any tension built up through the rotational muscles in the sides of the torso.

ROTATIONAL HIP STRETCH VAR. NO. 2

Purpose: To stretch the rotational lower back and buttock muscles and improve spinal mobility.

Prepare: Lie on your back with knees bent and arms stretched out in a T-position.

Perform: Drop your knees to one side and swing the top leg foot along the floor towards the opposite arm. Slide the leg back to the starting position. Alternate sides as you go through your repetitions.

Prudence: Shoulders remain in contact with the floor, neck relaxed.

Rotational hip stretch var. no. 2

SEATED BUTTOCK STRETCH VAR. NO 2

Purpose: To stretch the outer hip, buttock muscles and mid-back.

Prepare: Sit with your left leg bent over your right leg and the left foot flat on the floor by the right hip. Your right leg will be bent with your right foot on the floor outside of the left hip. Hook the right elbow around the left shin and place the left fingertips on the floor besides the left hip.

Perform: Press into the left hand and lift your spine up tall. Pull on your left leg with your right arm to turn the chest and head to the left. Stay for up to 10 deep breaths, and then release.

Prudence: Maintain an easeful effort and use the supporting hand to help keep the spine lifted and neutral and the shoulders down the back.

Finally, this abdominal stretch will open the front of the body to ward off any stooping forward that may occur due to tightness in this area.

ABDOMINAL STRETCH (SPHINX)

Purpose: To stretch the front of the body.

Prepare: Lie on your front.

Perform: Place the forearms with the elbows under the shoulders. Lift your chest towards the sky.

Prudence: Keep the back of the neck relaxed and draw the belly slightly in.

Your body should be feeling loosened off after these stretches, and ready to go again for the next run, whenever that may be.

Occasional extra release work for recovery after running

Although we used release work in preparation for running in this section, it would be remiss of us to not offer you some release exercises to deal with the tension built up during running over time. So, here are some extras for you to work on post-run alongside stretching. As discussed, release work can be used to check how the muscle tension in the body is feeling, to loosen off areas that may get chronically tight and to occasionally top up muscle pliability. As such, you might do this in the evening as part of your recovery or once a week or month, depending on your body's needs.

Running involves repetitively extending the hip, so it's important to release the buttock muscles that perform this movement. Here's how:

Release ball

BUTTOCK MUSCLES RELEASE VAR. NO. 5

Purpose: To release the buttock muscles.

Prepare: Sit with your knees bent and cross one ankle over the opposite knee.

Perform: Place a release ball under the buttock muscle on the lifted leg and support your weight with your hands. Remain on the ball for up to 10 breaths. Move the ball slightly to find a different spot in the buttock muscle, and repeat to explore and release the tension.

Prudence: Remain on muscle, not bone or joints.

The continuous pressing off the floor with the feet and lower leg muscles means that the lower calf muscle will need some releasing occasionally. We recommend this exercise:

Stool

LOWER LEG RELEASE VAR. NO. 3

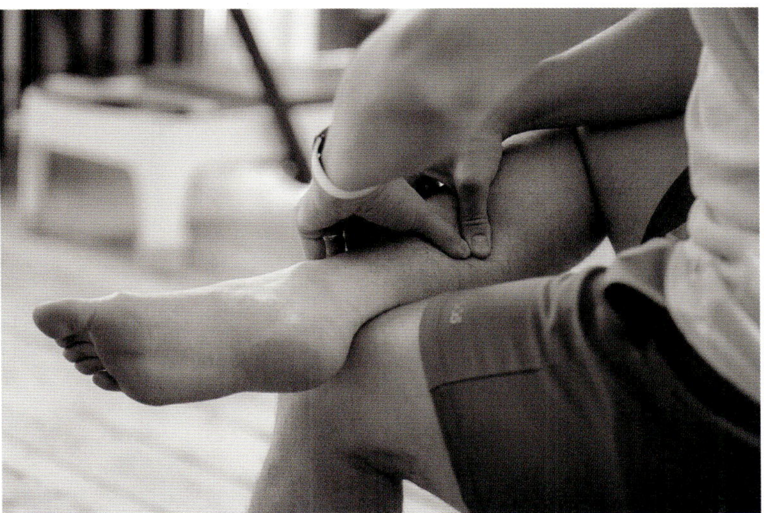

Purpose: To release deep lower leg muscles.

Prepare: Sit on a chair or stool with one ankle crossed over the opposite knee.

Perform: Use your thumbs to press into the muscles of the back of the lifted lower leg. Gradually work your way along the length of the muscles.

Prudence: Keep on the main bulk of the calf, below the knee and above the Achilles.

BACK EXTENSION MOBILISATION VAR. NO. 1 (RELEASE)

Purpose: To release the back muscles either side of the spine.

Prepare: Sit with the a roller behind you. Lie back, placing your mid-back onto the roller while holding the back of your head with your hands.

Perform: Extend your back over the roller, deepening the pressure in that area. Take 10 deep breaths and move 1cm up or down the spine to mobilise another area in the same way.

Prudence: Relax the neck.

By releasing these areas occasionally, it should reset your body to feel like you have a spring in your step on your next run!

Section 5

Applying 123 to swimming

This is our final model for an alternative way to use our 123 Approach for positive effect. As we hope you understand by this point, this model can be used flexibly. Our intention is to place emphasis on the need to combine 1 strength, 2 stretch and 3 release work as part of your preparation for, and recovery from, exercise. This will complete our offering of the ways you can think about, and integrate, these areas into your exercise routines.

This is our suggested 123 Approach model option for swimming:

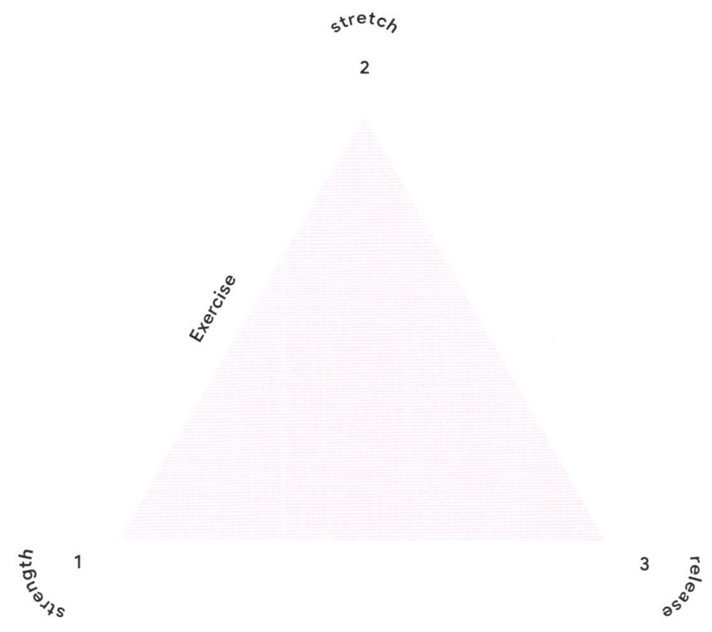

How reaching and rotating relate to swimming

To maintain our ability to reach and rotate without shoulder or back discomfort, we need to keep the spine and shoulders strong and mobile with a good range of motion in both areas. Swimming directly relates to these movements when considering a basic front crawl. This involves a full range of motion in the shoulder combined with a rotation in the torso when we breathe on either side in a freestyle stroke. The following programme progresses on from the reach and rotate section on page 88 as a preparation for this stroke. However, these exercises will apply well to breaststroke and backstroke as well.

Rotate and breath
Lats, hip flexors, core and arms

Head down and reach
Lats, hip flexors, core and arms

Reach and rotate
Obliques, shoulders, glutes

1 Strength

Swimming is a low-impact cardiovascular activity. What it gets away with in low impact it makes up for in difficulty of breathing. To get the correct muscles working in the body takes knowledge and application. However, once you understand and know how to achieve this, it frees you up to be able to focus on breathing. When executing a swim stroke efficiently, you only get to breathe when your head is out of the water. Knowing that the correct muscles are ready and working leaves one less thing to have to think about.

Spotlight: Muscles involved in swimming

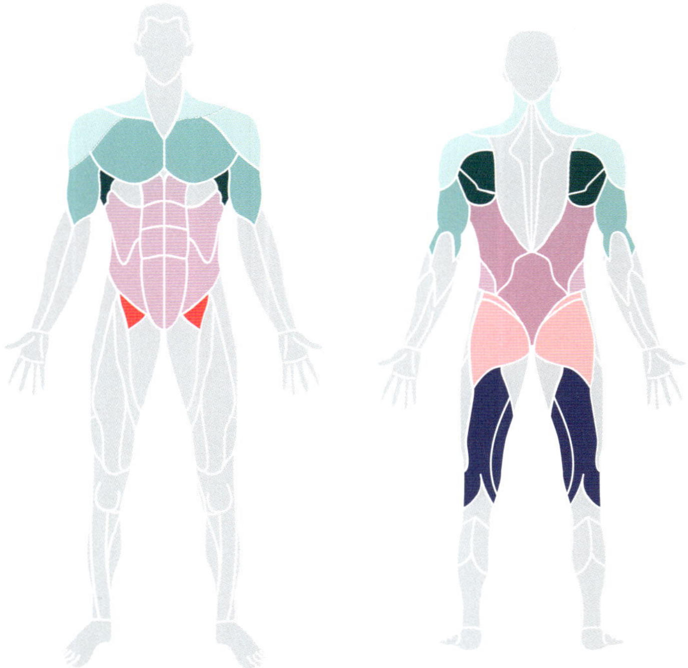

It's important to actively maintain good hip flexor activation and flexibility for swimming. This first exercise will get us connected to this idea and area of the body:

KNEE FLOATS VAR. NO. 4 (STRENGTH)

Purpose: To strengthen the deep core muscles.

Prepare: Lie on your back with your knees lifted directly above the hips and shins horizontal. Reach your arms straight up above your shoulders.

Perform: Pull the lower belly in. Simultaneously extend your arms and legs out on a diagonal line. Bring the arms and legs back to the start position.

Prudence: Move slowly and with control. Maintain a neutral lower back.

We will also be using the big muscles in the back that pull the water backwards to propel us forwards. This exercise will connect and activate this area in preparation for front crawl:

TheraBand

IN FRONT PULLS VAR. NO. 2 (STRENGTH)

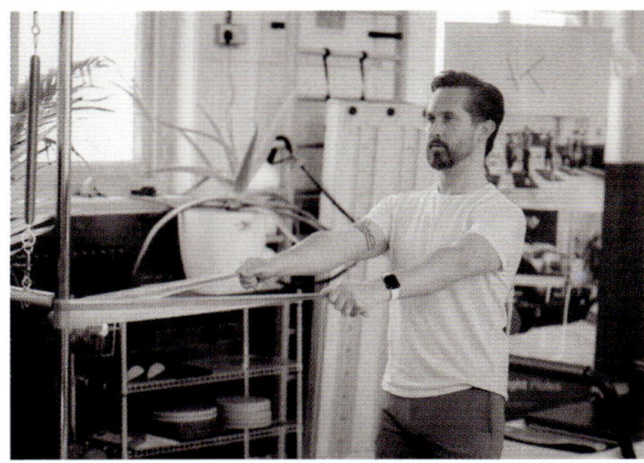

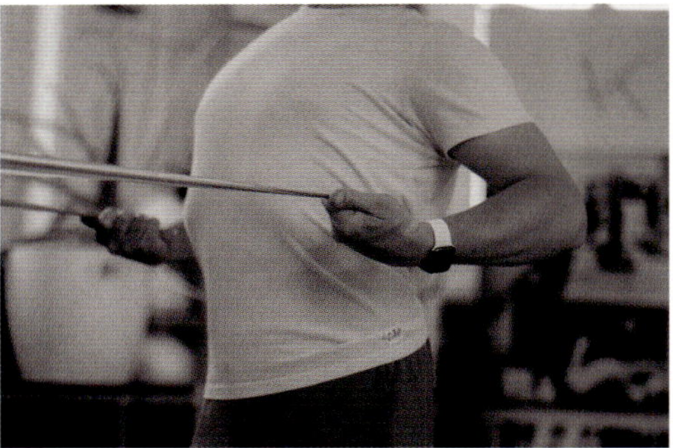

Purpose: To strengthen the areas below the shoulder blades and improve the shoulder blade connection to the back.

Prepare: Wrap the TheraBand around an immoveable surface. Stand with your feet hip distance apart and arms outstretched, taking hold of the ends of the TheraBand. Make sure that you have positioned yourself far enough away from the fixed point to have a little bit of tension in the band.

Perform: Pull your hands in towards you, rotating your palms up as you lift your breastbone, expanding the front of the ribs. Return your hands to the start position and relax the ribcage.

Prudence: Draw the shoulders down and elbows in and feel the back working.

Our legs extend at the hip, going behind the body, whilst we complete half the movement of a leg kick. Keeping the model on page 212 in mind, it's important to make this a conscious movement, to keep us in balance and not get 'top heavy' when swimming.

BUTTOCK PULSES (STRENGTH)

Purpose: To strengthen the buttock muscles.

Prepare: On all fours, making sure your hands are underneath the shoulders and knees underneath the hips, gently draw the stomach in to maintain a neutral spine. Turn the leg that is lifted out.

Perform: Lift one leg, keeping the angle of the knee at 90 degrees. Pulse the heel up and down to work into the buttock muscles.

Prudence: Keep the shoulder blades gently drawing down the back. Manage how high the leg lift is based on maintaining a neutral spine.

Good shoulder health means making use of several movements in the shoulder area. Pulls towards you overhead, as well as pulls towards you with arms at chest height, will go a long way to achieving this. Here is a good exercise to strengthen your shoulders:

SIDE WORK (STRENGTH)

Purpose: To strengthen the side of the core and the arms.

Prepare: Sit on your right side with your knees slightly bent, leaning onto the right palm. Your right hand, hips and feet should be in one line.

Perform: Push down on the right hand and stretch your legs, lifting the hips into a side plank position. Reach the left arm overhead, the same way your right fingers are facing. Return to the start position with control.

Prudence: Maintain the lift of the hips and stay in one line as if between 2 panes of glass.

This final exercise is to connect everything together. Here you have hip extension combined with hip stability. You will need to connect with the core and stabilise the spine. You are also working on shoulder strength and connecting the arms into the back.

PLANK WITH LEG LIFT PULSES (STRENGTH)

Purpose: Full body strengthening with a strong focus on the arms and core.

Prepare: Assume an all fours position with your shoulders over the wrists and hips above the knees.

Perform: Step your legs back one at a time into a plank position. Lengthen through the arms and slightly draw the tummy in. Lift one leg off the floor, being sure to keep the pelvis level and spine neutral. Pulse the lifted leg up and down for 30 seconds. Place the foot back on the floor and alternate sides as you go through your repetitions.

Prudence: Keep a light engagement of your abdominal muscles to maintain a neutral lower back.

Completing these exercises will leave you feeling ready to swim!

Go for a swim

2 Stretch

Swimming can leave your shoulders tight through all the arm movements you execute in any of the strokes. Swimming can also leave your mid-back tight from the excess breathing you need to keep a good pace and it may leave your lower back tight due to the hip flexor movements, as described in our spotlight on page 73. It is important to keep these areas loosened off to make sure that any tightness in these areas does not lead to joint issues and, therefore, chronic pain.

Spotlight: Muscles to stretch after swimming

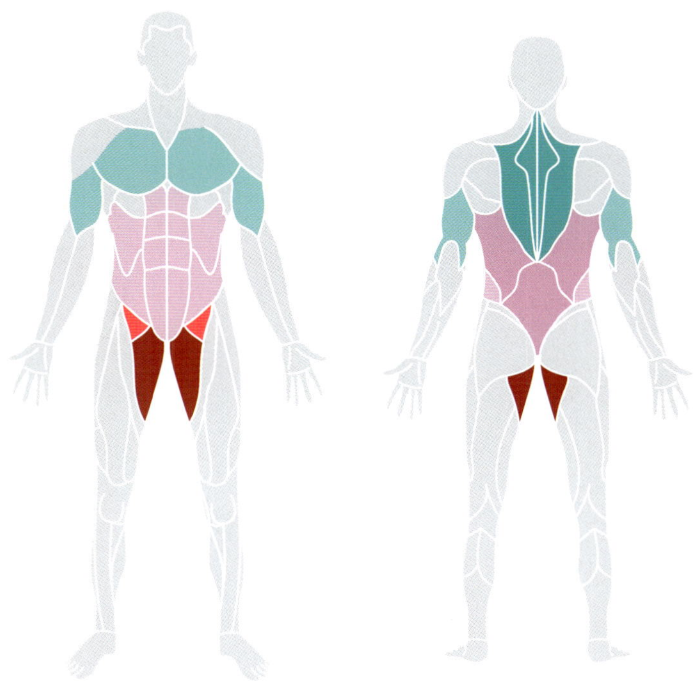

Post swim, the exercises in this section are designed to loosen off any tension developed in the spine. The exercises on pages 193, 197 and 200 can easily be done sitting poolside, and can be performed standing if there isn't a seat available.

Cushion

ROTATION SIDE LYING VAR. NO. 1 (STRETCH)

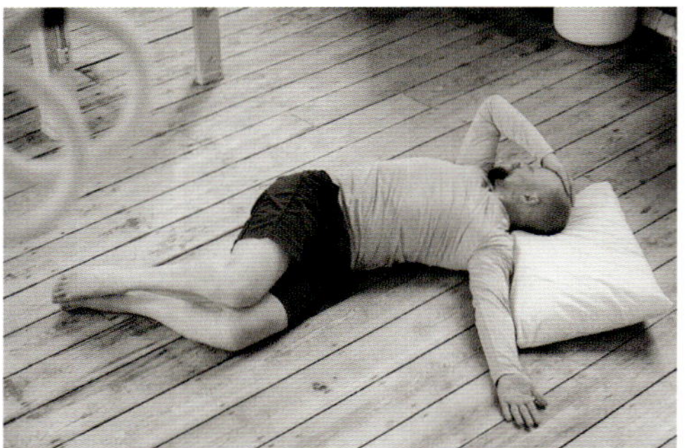

Purpose: To mobilise the spine and stretch the mid-back.

Prepare: Lie on your side with your knees slightly bent, the underneath arm stretched out in front of you and the top hand placed on your forehead. Support the head with a cushion.

Perform: Leading with the top elbow, rotate the upper body and head towards the opposite side. Rotate back to the starting position and repeat up to 10 times.

Prudence: Keep the pelvis still and the extended arm in contact with the floor.

LATERAL FLEXION STANDING (STRETCH)

Purpose: To stretch the side of the body and back of the upper arm.

Prepare: Stand with your feet hip width apart. Reach one arm up and take hold of the wrist with the opposite hand.

Perform: Lift in your waist and lean away from the extended arm, bringing the body into a side bend.

Prudence: Keep the pelvis level and facing forward, imagining you are standing in between 2 panes of glass.

This third exercise also releases out the spine while loosening off the underside of the shoulders at the same time. You may get away with using your towel poolside to place under the knees.

CHILD'S POSE VAR. NO. 2 (STRETCH)

Purpose: To stretch the back and encourage relaxation.

Prepare: Assume an all fours position with toes untucked.

Perform: Sit the buttocks back onto the heels, folding at the hips with the forehead on the floor. Place the back of the hands besides the hips and let the arms relax.

Prudence: Let the weight of the hips and head release.

Whether you have or haven't mixed up your stroke with some breaststroke added in, it's always a good thing to stretch the inner thighs when warm.

INNER THIGHS STRETCH

Purpose: To stretch the inner thighs.

Prepare: Sit with your legs out in a V shape.

Perform: Lift in the waist and reach both arms forwards as you lean your chest and body into the space in front of you.

Prudence: Keep the knees and toes facing the ceiling for maximum effect.

ROTATIONAL BUTTOCK STRETCH

Purpose: To stretch the outer hip, buttock muscles and front of shoulder and improve spinal mobility.

Prepare: Lie on your back, right leg straight and your right foot on top of the left thigh. Open the right arm in a T-position with the palm facing upwards. Reach the left hand across to take hold of the outer right thigh.

Perform: Use the left hand to pull the right leg across the body and towards the left shoulder, keeping the right arm connected to the floor.

Prudence: Relax the neck.

The shoulders are an easily forgotten about area of the body to stretch. Here are two stretches that will ensure the back and tops of the shoulders remain tension-free post-swim.

BACK OF UPPER ARM STRETCH VAR. NO. 1

Purpose: To stretch the back of the upper arm.

Prepare: Stand or sit upright.

Perform: Place one hand between the shoulder blades and take hold of that elbow with the other one, keeping the elbows facing towards the ceiling.

Prudence: Don't be afraid to use a belt if your hands don't reach.

BETWEEN SHOULDER STRETCH

Purpose: To stretch the back of the shoulders.

Prepare: Assume a child's pose and take hold of the heels with your fingers facing your toes.

Perform: Keeping hold of your feet, roll forwards onto the top of your head.

Prudence: Straighten your arms as you press forwards into the space between the shoulder blades.

The front of the thighs and hip will tighten up from the second half of the leg kick movement. These next two stretches will loosen these closely connected areas off.

FRONT OF THIGH STRETCH VAR. NO. 2

Purpose: To stretch the front of the thighs.

Prepare: Sit on the floor with the legs outstretched in front.

Perform: Lean over to the left, taking your weight onto the left hand. Bend your right knee and place the right foot beside the right hip. Bring your weight back onto both buttocks and lean back onto your elbows.

Prudence: Maintain a good awareness of how your bent knee feels. If you are experiencing knee discomfort, seek advice.

LOW LUNGE VAR. NO. 3 (STRETCH)

Purpose: To strengthen and stretch the front of the hip and thigh, stretch the back and improve your balance.

Prepare: Start by standing with plenty of space around you. Step into a lunge position with your right leg forwards and left leg back. Place the left elbow onto the right thigh. Place the right hand on top of the left hand, with the right elbow pointing towards the ceiling.

Perform: Turn the chest slightly to the right. Lengthen the spine, press the right hand into the left and turn the chest and head to the right. Stay for several breaths. Look down to the floor and step back to standing.

Prudence: Keep your front knee stacked over the front ankle.

3 Release

Hopefully you are now feeling looser and taller with a free and easy spine after swimming! This is the beauty of this great cardiovascular activity that has next to zero impact going through your joints. Swimming also works almost all of the muscles in the body.

This series of releases is likely to be performed at home. As such, it might be one to be done in the evening, so the workout doesn't extend to take up too much of a time slot in your day. Either way, this addresses the areas that will need releasing post-swim or just occasionally if you are a regular swimmer. When releasing the back, it is important to separate the lower, mid and upper areas, as they need slightly different techniques for each.

Spotlight: Muscles to release after swimming

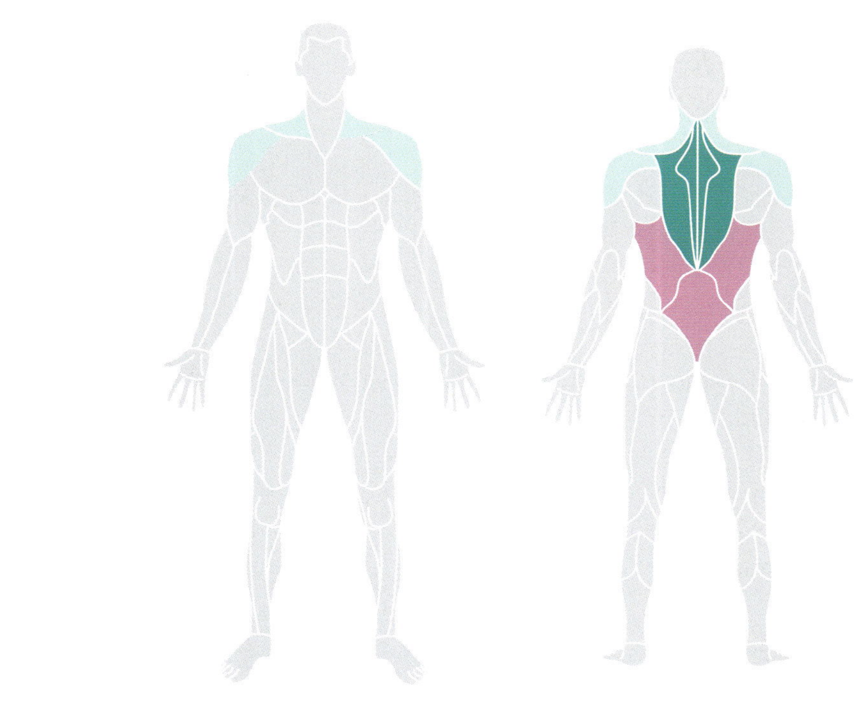

BACK EXTENSION MOBILISATION VAR. NO. 2 (RELEASE)

Purpose: To release the back muscles either side of the spine.

Prepare: Sit with the roller behind you. Lie back, placing the mid-back onto the roller while holding the back of your head with your hands.

Perform: Extend your back over the roller and slowly rotate the head and chest over to one side, deepening the pressure in that area. Alternate sides as you go through your repetitions.

Prudence: Fully support the head weight in your hands to maintain a relaxed neck.

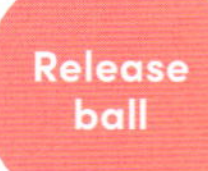

TUCKED PELVIS LOWER BACK RELEASE

Purpose: To release the muscles of the lower back. This area can tighten and overwork if your side body isn't in good condition.

Prepare: Lie in a constructive rest position. Place a release ball underneath the lower back on one side. Start just below the ribs.

Perform: Draw the stomach in and tuck the pelvis slightly, imprinting your back into the ball. Stay for up to 10 breaths, then move 1cm down the lower back and repeat. Continue down your spine until you reach your pelvis.

Prudence: Stay off any bones, especially the spine.

Releasing the upper back and shoulders can benefit from raised hips to give you an angle on an area of the body that curves away from the floor when you are on your back.

Roller + release balls

SHOULDER BLADE RELEASE

Purpose: To release the muscles on the inside of the shoulder blades.

Prepare: Lie in a constructive rest position. Place a release ball underneath either side of the shoulders. Lift the hips off the ground and place a roller underneath the sacrum.

Perform: Cross your arms to bring your hands to the opposite shoulders and roll back and forth, massaging the shoulders and between the shoulder blades.

Prudence: Make sure the balls are on muscle, avoiding the spine.

This next exercise will release the area on the top of the shoulders. This area can get tight and build up tension, feeling uncomfortable, particularly if you are in a seated office job.

Roller + release balls

UPPER SHOULDER RELEASE VAR. NO. 2

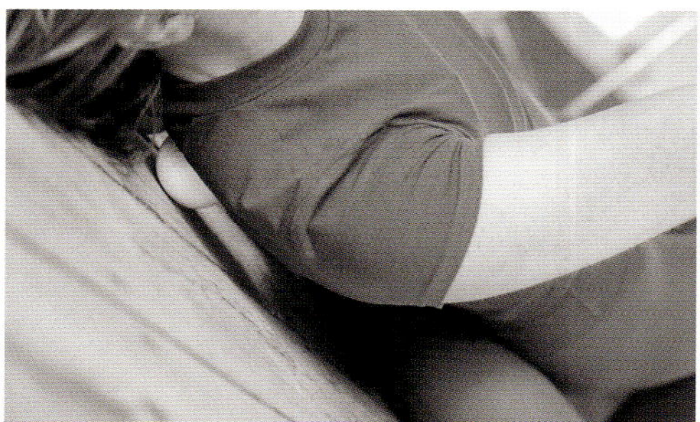

Purpose: To release the upper shoulders.

Prepare: Lie in a constructive rest position. Place a release ball underneath either side of your shoulders. Lift your hips off the ground and place a roller underneath your sacrum.

Perform: Slowly raise your arms over your head onto the floor. Take 10 deep breaths. Bring the arms back up, move to a slightly different spot and repeat.

Prudence: Place the roller carefully so your lower back feels supported. Make sure the massage balls are placed on the muscles either side of your spine away from the spine itself.

This set of releases should leave you feeling loose in your back and shoulders after a swim. Do not forget to do something for your legs on another day to keep a good general body balance, as laid out in the Triangle model of the body that follows on page 212.

Section

Taking things forward

Applying the 123 Approach to different movement forms

What we have already covered will hopefully have given you a perspective on how you might apply the 123 Approach to other movements. By now you will be feeling confident that you know exercises to activate muscles, stretch muscles out and release muscles off.

Using what you know, you can now embark on discovering and experimenting with utilising the information in this book. We have shown you how to develop strategies to deal with the tension generated by your chosen activities.

We are also planning follow-up books to look at some specific activities that we feel would benefit from a bit more information. However, here are some things to consider when approaching this on your own:

- **Look at the overall movement,** such as running motion.
- **Break it down into its component parts** – hip extension, pressing off the foot, twist in body and arm movements.
- **Identify what muscles are involved** – buttocks, back of thigh, rotational waist muscles and shoulders.
- **Apply the 123 Approach to those muscles** – how do you strengthen, stretch and release those muscles.
- **Consider what model of the 123 Approach will best fit (see pages 103–105)** – strength exercise stretch release / release strength exercise stretch / strength exercise stretch downtime release.

We would encourage you to get curious about your own body and experiment with the techniques described in this book with different activities. Life is better when we move, and we move better when we have variety in our activities!

Applying the 123 Approach to gym work

Our advice for gym users is to utilise these exercises to work on what muscles to engage before you start moving or lifting. The areas we would advise paying particular attention to are as follows:

- Deep abdominal exercises to support the spine.
- Lower gluteal activation before performing any kind of press with the legs.
- Shoulder blade connection to back as a complement to upper shoulder and arm development.
- Feet and lower leg focus to balance overwork in the thighs.

We would also recommend staying on top of your stretching and release work in the following way:

- Upper shoulder and upper back releasing and stretching after arm work.
- Maintain a mobile and flexible spine rotationally, laterally and in flexion.
- Back of thighs and hips stretching and releasing after any leg work.
- Hip flexors and outside of hips and thighs releasing and stretching after leg work.

We also want to give you a practical way of working the upper torso for when you cannot make it to the gym. Next is a fun and approachable exercise for that, combined with another model to aid your decisions and thought processes.

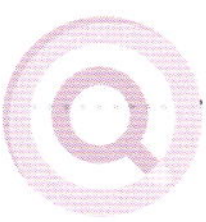

Spotlight: The triangle model of the body

At this stage we wanted to introduce a concept diagram that we have found useful. We call this our 'triangle model of the body'. We use the triangle shape to emphasise our perspective that most of your strength and stability work should be in the lower half of your body. This is aided by working on your core muscles to stabilise your lower spine and pelvis. We believe arm work should have a very specific focus on functional stability with an emphasis on range of motion and reduced neck and shoulder tension. This combines with the goals of core stability and leg work to aid spinal mobility, resulting in a versatility of movement patterns.

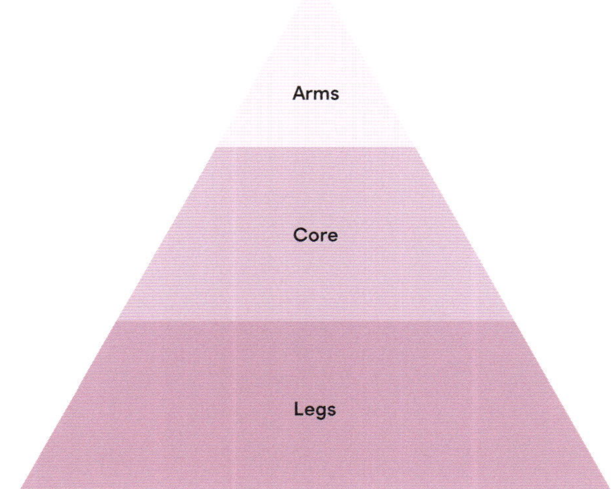

If you think about the shape of the human body, you will notice that the legs are the largest and longest of the limbs. That means they have the most potential for strength, stability and power. That said, they can take a lot of tension.

The shoulders, on the other hand, suffer with excess tension when we overload them. The arms are designed for reaching and grasping. They are imbued with a range of motion, which is important to maintain. As a result, they are at their best when dealing with less strengthening work, or load, but increased range of movement. If we keep in mind a general goal of vitality within our bodies, then it is important to take the idea of striving for balance seriously. That means appropriate work in the appropriate areas. So, rather than 'bulking up' in the upper torso, we suggest the following exercises to keep the shoulders strong but not out of balance!

Applying the 123 Approach to a handstand

One way of getting a good amount of shoulder strength, without bulking up, is to practise a handstand. This also gives you the extra benefits of taking pressure off the vertebrae joints in the spine, potentially helps clear the lymph system and improves blood circulation. So, let us put the 123 Approach into practice by looking at a **handstand**. Here is what the 123 Approach for a handstand exercise looks like mapped out together:

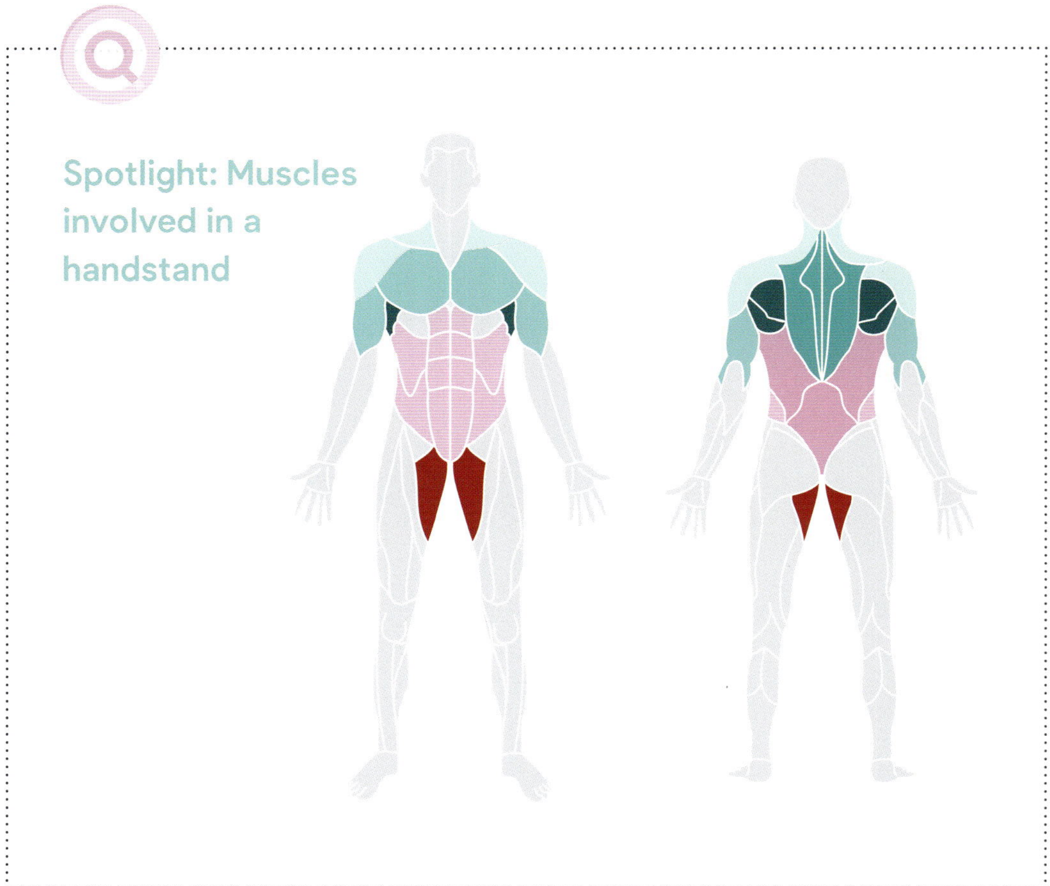

It is important to begin a movement where you transfer your full body weight onto the arms by warming up the wrists, like this:

Support

WRIST STRETCH

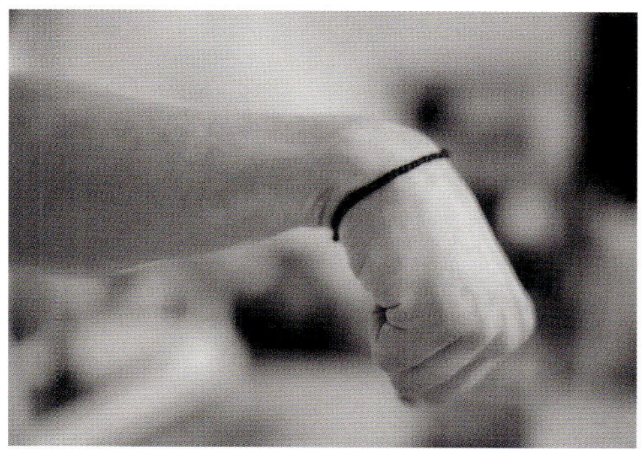

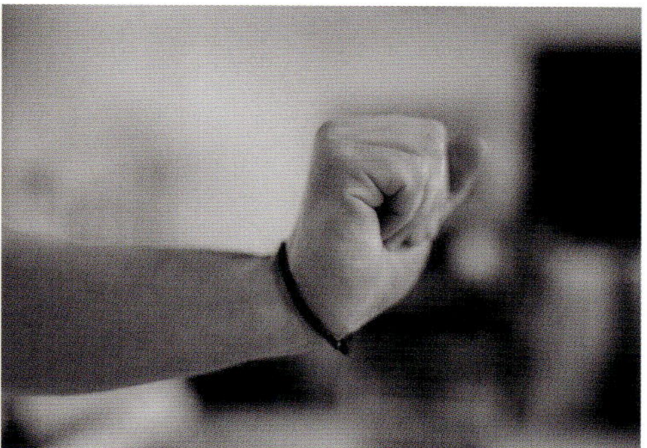

Purpose: To stretch and warm up the wrists.

Prepare: Reach the arms out in front of you at shoulder height.

Perform: Make a fist and flex and extend the wrists. Repeat 10 times back and forth.

Prudence: Go slowly to begin with and build range.

These next two exercises will help you to engage the core, which will allow you to keep the whole body working as one, resulting in improved balance.

SIDE STANDING (STRENGTH)

Purpose: To work the sides of the waist.

Prepare: Stand about a foot away from a hip-height support (for example, a kitchen work area). Place the foot of the leg nearest the surface so that it is aligned with and in front of the other foot. Lift the outside arm up and place the inside arm in front of the waist.

Perform: Lift in the waist and laterally flex the torso towards the surface you are leaning on. Return to upright.

Prudence: Keep the hips and shoulders facing forward and avoid twisting.

DOUBLE LEG STRETCH (STRENGTH)

Purpose: To strengthen the core muscles.

Prepare: Lie on your back and take hold of your knees. Lift your head and shoulders off the floor.

Perform: Simultaneously stretch the arms and legs out on opposite diagonals. Bring the arms and legs back into the start position. Try some with your head down to focus on the lower abdominals more.

Prudence: Keep the legs at a reasonable height so as not to make it too difficult to keep the lower back in the same position as you started in.

This next exercise will ensure the other side of the body, the back, is engaged, so these areas can co-contract to find a balance of the body in space, which a handstand demands.

ARROW VAR. NO. 3 (STRENGTH)

Purpose: To strengthen the upper back.

Prepare: Lie down on your stomach and place your hands on the floor beside the hips, with the palms facing upwards.

Perform: Lift your arms off the floor and draw the shoulder blades down your back as you lift the head and shoulders off the floor about an inch or two. Stay lifted and raise one leg off the floor as a variation. Lower the whole body back down and repeat on the other leg.

Prudence: Keep the back of the neck long; only a small lift of the legs.

This next exercise will warm up the shoulders, back of the thighs and lengthen out the back.

DOWNWARD DOG (STRETCH)

Purpose: To stretch the back of the legs, decompress the spine and strengthen the arms and shoulders.

Prepare: Begin on all fours with your toes tucked under.

Perform: Send your hips back and up as you straighten the legs out. Press into the index fingers' thumb joint. Broaden the shoulders and upper back.

Prudence: Bend your knees or straighten the legs depending on your flexibility levels.

Here we have added an extra stretch for the back of the thighs to ensure they are loose enough to perform the kick part of getting the legs into a handstand position.

Strap

BACK OF THIGH STRETCH VAR. NO. 3

Purpose: To stretch the outside and back of the leg.

Prepare: Lie on your back with your legs straight and the strap within reach.

Perform: Raise the right leg and place the strap over the ball of the foot. Hold the ends of the strap with both hands. Extend the right leg up to the sky, flexing the right foot. Take both ends of the strap in your left hand and place the right hand on the right hip. Pull the right leg slightly across the body to the left.

Prudence: Keep the right hip on the floor and the spine neutral.

This is a great way to prep for a handstand without committing to it, or the possibility of going head over heels.

BUNNY HOP (STRENGTH)

Purpose: Full body strengthening that warms the body up. Learning what it feels like to balance the pelvis over the shoulders.

Prepare: Crouch down and place the hands on the floor shoulder-width apart, looking between the hands.

Perform: Use the legs to spring the hips up into the air until the hips are roughly over the shoulders.

Prudence: Maintain a neutral spine by engaging the core.

HANDSTAND (STRENGTH)

Purpose: To strengthen the arms and shoulders. Learn how to balance upside down.

Prepare: Place the hands on the floor around 5cm away from a wall, with your legs in a runner's sprint start position.

Perform: Use your legs to send the hips over the shoulders by kicking one leg towards the wall, followed in quick succession by the other leg. Slightly squeeze the inner thighs and reach up through the legs.

Prudence: Engage the core and keep the spine neutral.

You should feel ready now to go into a handstand movement against a wall.

Do a handstand

These next three exercises will ensure you have released any tension built up in the spine by rotating, laterally flexing and curving the back.

Cushion

ROTATION SIDE LYING VAR. NO. 2 (STRETCH)

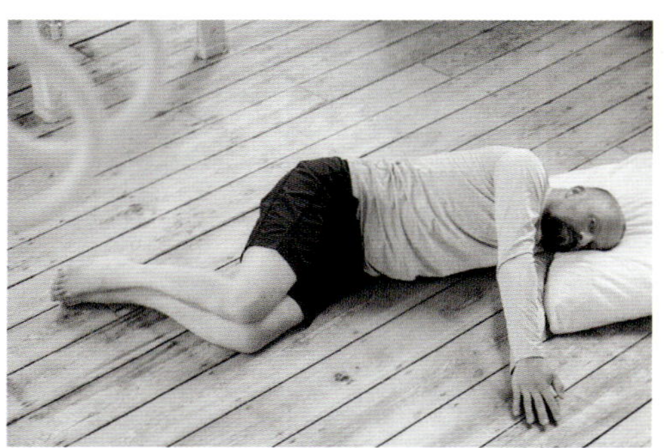

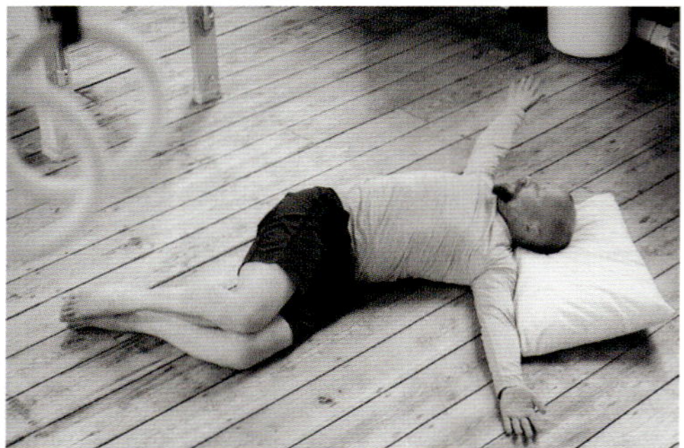

Purpose: To mobilise the spine and stretch the mid-back.

Prepare: Lie on your side with your knees slightly bent and arms stretched out in front of you. Use a cushion to support your head.

Perform: Leading with your top arm, rotate the upper body and head towards the opposite side. Rotate back to the starting position and repeat several times.

Prudence: Keep the pelvis still and the underneath arm in contact with the floor.

LATERAL STRETCH STANDING

Purpose: To stretch the spine and back laterally.

Prepare: Stand on your right foot with your left foot against the right thigh, knee pointing out to the side. Reach the right arm up and relax the left arm by your side.

Perform: Lean your upper body over to the left coming into a side bend, with the back of the left hand on the left thigh. Come back to neutral spine and release the left foot down.

Prudence: Go directly to the side as if between 2 panes of glass. Keep your weight evenly spread across the standing foot.

CAT STRETCH VAR. NO. 3

Purpose: To stretch the back and mobilise the spine.

Prepare: Assume an all fours position with your hands wider than shoulder width, and slightly in front of the shoulders this time.

Perform: Draw the navel in and round the back. Return to a neutral spine. Repeat several times.

Prudence: Relax the back of the neck.

These next three exercises will stretch out the shoulders to maintain reduced tension, whilst building strength and stability with a handstand.

THREAD THE NEEDLE (STRETCH)

Purpose: To stretch the back of the shoulder.

Prepare: Assume an all fours position.

Perform: Reach the right arm underneath the left arm, bending the left elbow and bringing the right arm and shoulder onto the floor. Press the hips slightly back. Push the left hand down to turn the chest to the left. Return to all fours. Repeat several times, alternating sides as you progress.

Prudence: Rest your head on the floor and relax the neck.

BACK OF UPPER ARM STRETCH VAR. NO. 2

Purpose: To stretch the back of the upper arm.

Prepare: Stand or sit upright with or without a strap or belt.

Perform: Place one hand between the shoulder blades and take hold of it with the other one, keeping that latter elbow facing towards the ceiling. If you can reach without a strap, link the hands instead.

Prudence: Don't be afraid to use a strap or belt if your hands don't reach.

EAGLE ARMS VAR. NO.2 (STRETCH)

Purpose: To stretch the back of the shoulders. We have chosen sitting cross legs as a variation to include hip mobility and back strengthening.

Prepare: Sit with your legs crossed.

Perform: Cross one elbow on top of the other. With the hand of the underneath arm, take hold of the opposite thumb. Lift the elbows to shoulder height. Press the elbows forwards and slightly squeeze the forearms into each other.

Prudence: Keep the head and neck in a neutral position as your elbows gently press forwards.

Finally, it's a good idea to keep up with your upper shoulder releases when performing more strenuous exercises for the upper torso, like the handstand.

Roller + release ball

UPPER SHOULDER RELEASE VAR. NO. 3

Purpose: To release the upper shoulders.

Prepare: Lie in a constructive rest position. Place a release ball underneath one side of the shoulders and reach the arms as if hugging a big ball. Lift the hips off the ground and place a roller underneath the sacrum.

Perform: Rotate 70% of your weight onto one side. Take 10 deep breaths before finding another spot and tracking your discomfort.

Prudence: Place the roller carefully so the lower back feels supported. Make sure the balls are placed on the muscles either side of the spine, away from the spine itself.

To summarise, this sequence should leave you feeling strong and flexible in the shoulders, and confident that you can support your body weight in this most challenging of functional positions for the arms.

Section

Further thoughts

Well done for working through our thoughts and exercises. We realise there is a lot here to digest and utilise. A strength of our sharing we feel! Our hope is that this will be of immense value to you when approaching exercise, whether you use this book as an exercise programme or you use our ideas to support other exercise choices.

We will leave you with a few closing thoughts. We believe mindset is of upmost importance, hence the models we lay out here in this book. An analogy we could offer is that it is a little bit like jazz. To make it look easy, you need some sound theory and structure in place to progress and thrive. We hope this journey with your body will leave you progressing and thriving in a sustainable way. That means injury free, responsive to your relationship with your body, and being able to be creative with where to take things next!

Walking the middle way with the 123 Approach

Making sure we don't over exercise and optimising rest periods seem to us to be just as important as making sure we keep up our motivation to exercise in the first place. Different bodies will need different levels of activity, rest, stretching, strengthening and releasing. We believe the best chance you can give someone towards achieving this balance is by helping them connect with, and maintain the relationship with, their own body. Imagine a tightrope, where achieving this balance means staying on. On one side you could fall into the trap of not exercising enough. On the other side, you could fall into the trap of over exercising. The trick is to get listening to your body and get the balance right.

Listening to your body and geting the balance right

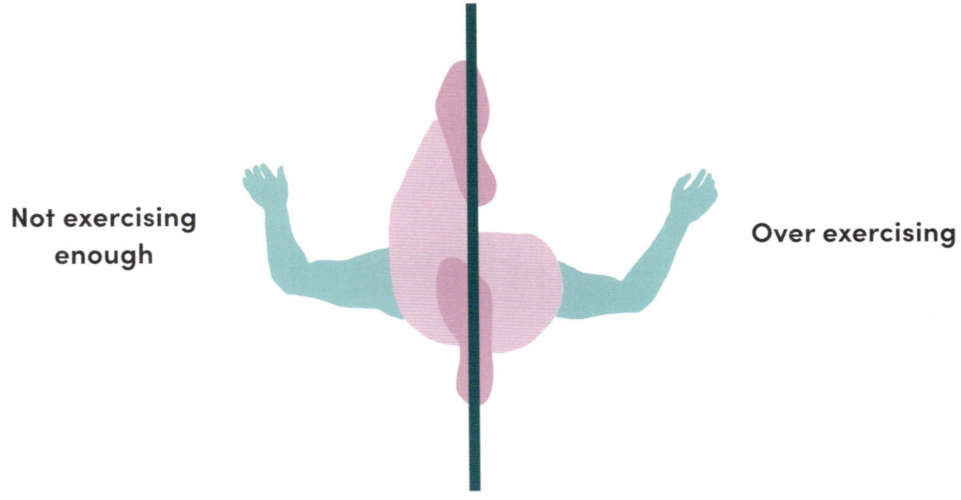

How do you develop your physical intelligence?

One of the real benefits about holistic approaches to the body, as in Pilates and Yoga, is developing body awareness. This means that we listen to our bodies and don't make exercises a pre-set idea based on unrealistic goals.

As well as working towards an aesthetic, an unrealistic goal also includes deciding we want to go for a 15-mile run because we want to get fit. A more sensible strategy might be running until your body says it has had enough, and slowly developing your stamina in response to how much your body tells you it can cope with. If the former happens on an ongoing basis, it can lead to fatigue and overuse of certain muscles and joints, which in turn can lead to injury. Work on the latter and you give yourself the opportunity to develop lasting body enjoyment achieved in collaboration with your body's natural intelligence and instincts.

The 'Holy Grail' of minimising workouts

When it comes to conditioning work, we believe that it is at its best when specific and tailored. As such, we would recommend that you experiment with the exercises in this book and work out a programme that suits you. Then strip it down to what is essential over time. There will be a bare minimum that your body needs to keep you moving well, remaining flexible, strong and relaxed. Then you'll be ready to go whenever you need or want to. Whether it's skiing in the Alps in winter, going for a walk with a friend or deciding to sign up for a marathon, you will be in the right place in your body with knowledge of the 123 Approach.

The importance of variety

As you continue to progress on this new journey with your body, one thing we would recommend is keeping things varied. Bodies like a range of movement patterns to remain in good shape. In professional sport, exercise programmes are periodised, meaning they only stick to one set of exercises for a certain number of weeks. We like to think of exercise like cooking, in that it's good to think seasonally. Hitting the gym in the winter may work well because it's indoors. Why not try open water swimming in the summer? Maybe some cycling in spring will allow you to visit as many parks as possible, whilst running in the autumn will keep you cool and outdoors for as long as possible. Whichever way you choose, keep up your 123 Approach to exercise and you'll be on the right track! We would also love to hear about the ways you are combining the areas we have put forward, so please get in touch!

Our training programme for instructors

Twice a year we run a training programme for our 123 Approach. This consist of 50 hours of in-person training over a 6-month period. During this training, you can either delve into our 123 Approach in more detail to be able to instruct others, or you can just enhance your knowledge, gaining support from us as you do so. Please get in touch if you would like more information.

Use this space to add any notes

We would like to thank:

Our wives, Jodie and Aimiee, for putting up with us throughout this process.

Our families, friends and clients for their continued support and enthusiasm.

Any colleagues and teachers for generously engaging with our ideas and sharing theirs.

Drew, for his photography.

Emily, for her design work and general guidance.

Rob, for his filming.

Diana, Dimitris and Joelle for their modelling.

Kay for her editing.

Graham, Karen and Richard for their quotes.

Michael for his efforts and belief in trying to find us a publisher.

Arran would like to thank his father, Richard, for his guidance and support with his writing.

And his newest inspiration and teacher, his daughter Petra.

We appreciate you all for helping us to bring this book into existence!

Follow us

/arranknightpilates
/DavidMichelYoga

@akpilates
@davidmichelyoga

www.arranknightpilates.com